HTML5 & CSS3
For Beginners
Your Guide To Easily Learn HTML5 &
CSS3 Programming in 7 Days

By iCode Academy

TABLE OF CONTENTS

INTRODUCTION:

Welcome to this training for the Kindle edition of "HTML5 & CSS3 For Beginners: Your Guide To Easily Learn HTML5 & CSS3 Programming in 24 Hours".

This book contains the steps, strategies, and information you need to learn HTML5 and CSS3, the latest and current standard languages for creating websites and designing web pages. It was conceptualized and developed to help beginners, business owners, and interested web users master the powerful features of these website creation and styling tools in as fast as one day.

Beginners and experienced web developers alike will find this practical book an enjoyable and reliable resource for learning the two hottest languages in website creation and design on their own. If you're planning to launch a lucrative career in web development, learning HTML5 and CSS3 through this learning material is the easiest, fastest, and least expensive way to start.

This visual-aided instruction material is a step-by-step guide to help you make use of the available tools, layout styles, built-in effects, and designing features of HTML5 and CSS3. It presents the precise steps and the image of the outcome after performing the steps. It will guide you from the very first step in website creation to the task of styling your web pages to make it attractive and pleasing to you and your visitors.

HTML is a mark-up language used to create web pages. An HTML code provides the structure and layout of a web page and instructs the web browsers what to display and how to present the text, images, videos, and sounds to viewers. HTML5, its latest version, is a backward-compatible language with many new and outstanding features that are supported and used by the major browsers such as Chrome, Internet Explorer, Firefox, Safari, and Opera.

HTML5 is an easy-to-learn website creation tool that uses concise syntax and flexible code structure. This book presents the tools, options, and features of HTML5 and shows how you can use them to create a visually attractive and user-friendly website. It features images to show the tools and the outcome of the steps. You will never get lost as you try out each code and explore its elements and properties.

The step-by-step guide provided in this book will show you how you can use free and simple text editors to write and run your own HTML code. It provides the instruction and the information you need to write your code accurately and take advantage of the many powerful features of HTML5.

The book includes standard references that you can read to learn about and make full use of the capabilities of HTML5 and CSS3. It presents quick guides to the most commonly used attribute, properties and their possible values and provides relevant examples to illustrate the topics. The chapters are strategically arranged to help you build the required skills as you proceed.

CSS, or Cascading Style Sheets, is the language used to describe how web pages should be presented, including its layout, fonts, and colors. It allows you to adapt your presentation to multiple devices such as large screens, portable devices, printers, or small screens. It is an independent web styling tool that can be used with HTML and other XML-based mark-up language.

CSS3 is the latest version of CSS and the current standard for web designing. It features webpage styling features and effects that will help you create visually stunning websites. Many of its features are intended to replace the styling features that were removed from the earlier versions of HTML to simplify website creation and layout codes.

If you are a website or business owner, you will want to use a web designing tool like CSS3 to ensure that your website is highly accessible, will remain usable in the future, truly responsive, and uses the industry standard in web designing. CSS3 is the fastest way to help you create a professional online presence that is consistent with your present brand.

While many content management systems can provide built-in themes and options for customizing them, learning CSS3 will empower you to step out of the box and create more personal and unique themes that don't look like everyone else's.

Like HTML5, CSS3 is an easy-to-learn language that you can master in a few hours. This learning material will show you how to create simple codes that you can use repeatedly to style multiple websites across different devices.

You will find different options for styling your web pages and decide which one works best for your needs or combine them all to create and provide a truly different and highly personalized website.

The instructions presented in this learning material book will show you how to use the simplest text editors to write CSS codes. It provides the precise steps and the information you need to write your code accurately and take advantage of the many powerful features and new built-in effects of CSS3. It contains images that will demonstrate the tool and the results of applying the styling features.

CSS3 is not just great for designing your website. It features several animation properties that you can apply to create plug in-free animations and build interactive interfaces. If you're planning to build a motion-based website, CSS offers an efficient solution that requires less than a day to learn and master.

The book "HTML5 & CSS3 For Beginners: Your Guide To Easily Learn HTML5 & CSS3 Programming in 24 Hours" is the ultimate resource for self-learners, students, and anyone who's interested in learning web designing for fun, business, and profit.

It is a useful reference material for web developers and digital marketers who want to learn and use the latest features of both HTML5 and CSS3.

This book is for beginners who want to start a freelance career in web designing at a fraction of the cost of studying computer science or other programming languages.

It is highly recommended for website owners who want to improve their digital presence by creating and designing a website that is attractive, web-friendly, and user-friendly.

CHAPTER 1: INTRODUCTION TO HTML

WHAT IS HTML?

HTML is an acronym for HyperText Markup Language. It is a standardized system for providing the layout, structure, and format of a web page. An HTML file tells the web browser how to display your web pages. HTML5 is the latest version of HTML and the new standard for web browsers. Its features include the following:

- New HTML elements an attributes
- Audio and video elements for media playback
- 2D and 3D graphics
- New form controls such as url, search, time, calendar, and date
- Local SQL database
- Local storage

HTML Text Editors

An HTML editor is a software application that you will need to create your web pages. Since it only requires a text file saved in ASCII format, you can use any text editing program to write your HTML codes. The following are the most commonly used HTML editors:

Text Editor	MS Windows Notepad
	Apple Mcintosh TextEdit
HTML Editors	Microsoft Expression
	Adobe Dreamweaver
Word Processing Program	MS Word

DocType

A DocType is a document declaration that defines the document type. The browser requires this information to process the HTML document and display the web page correctly.

HTML5 uses a simple DocType, <!DOCTYPE>, to distinguish an HTML5 document from other versions of HTML and from other documents submitted to the browser.

Metadata

Metadata is a set of data that provides information about another data. The data are not meant to be displayed on the web page but they make working with the instance of data easier by providing important information. They are placed in the head part of the HTML document and they are commonly used to specify information such as keywords, page description, and author.

Following are the elements of a metadata:

head   Defines a collection of metadata for the document
       Example: <head>...</head>

title Defines the document's name or title
       Example: <title>DogHouse</title>

base   Specifies the base URL for relative URLs
       <base href="http://www.DogHouse.com/news/index.html">

link   Defines the relationship of the document to an external
resource
       <link rel="company number" href="/about">

meta   Defines metadata that cannot be expressed using the other
elements

style Allows the author to specify the style information for a
page
       <style type="text/css"></style>
       <style><body> {color:blue; background:yellow;}</style></body>

Writing a Simple HTML Page

You can use any text editor but this training uses notepad as the text editor.

To create an HTML document, open the notepad and type the following data:

```
<!DOCTYPE html>
<html>
  <head>
    <title>Dog Care</title>
  </head>
  <body>
    Dog Care is a website for dog lovers who only want the best for their canine
friends.
  </body>
</html>
```

Saving an HTML File

After creating the document, you should save it for viewing or modifying later. When saving, remember to use either .html or .htm as file extension and change the file type to All Files.

Viewing the HTML Page

To view the page, launch a web browser. Go to the folder where the file is saved and right click on the file. Choose the option 'open with' and click your browser. The web page will display the contents you have enclosed within the body tags. If you make any modifications to the file, you must refresh or reload the page to apply and view the changes.

This is how the web page will look:

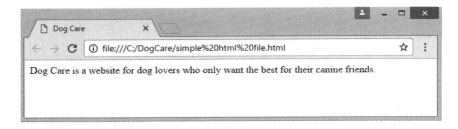

You Can Learn HTML and CSS in One Day

HTML is a simple language that you can learn in less than one day. It uses syntax and style that is easy to learn. It does not impose indentation and is not case-sensitive. Once you know the basic syntax, you can already create a decent webpage. You can add the special features and effects later to make the webpage attractive.

How to Use This Book to Learn HTML5 and CSS3 in One Day

To learn HTML and CSS in one day, this book presents code examples for each feature as well as tabular guide for the different elements and acceptable values. You can experiment on the code, modify them according to your needs, and create a code on your own.

The examples given in this book are indented to help beginners understand how the different sections of the code and the elements relate to each other. Indentation also makes the code easier to read.

The best way to learn is to read each chapter in the order in which they are presented in the book. In HTML, an element can have several attributes and these are presented on tables for reference. You can read them briefly for information. The most commonly used ones are discussed. You can focus on these discussions and the examples given.

CHAPTER 2: ELEMENTS, ATTRIBUTES, AND VALUES

HTML has three main mark-up components:

- Elements
- Attributes
- Values

Elements

An HTML element refers to everything that can be found from the start tag to the end tag, including the tags. Elements most commonly appear with a start tag, end tag, and the content between these tags. Here's an example:

<start tag>Content</end tag>

Empty HTML Elements

Some HTML elements have no content and they are called empty elements. An example is the <br> element which is used to define a line break. In addition, the <br> element has no closing tag.

What are Tags?

Tags are the building blocks of an HTML document. They are used to define how the browser must format and display the content. Tags commonly have two parts: opening and closing. The opening and closing tags are enclosed in angle brackets. In addition, the closing tag is introduced by a backslash.

Example: opening tag: <html>
             closing tag: </html>

The following tables present the different HTML Tags:

Tag	Function
<!DOCTYPE>	Defines document type
<html> </html>	Encloses the entire HTML document
<head> </head>	Encloses the head of the HTML document
<title> </title>	Indicates the document title
<body> </body>	Encloses the body of the HTML document
<p> </p>	Creates a paragraph
<hr>	Creates a horizontal line rule

	Creates a single line break
<ol>	Defines an ordered list
<ul>	Defines an unordered list
<h1> </h1>	Creates a first level heading
<h2> </h2>	Creates a second level heading
<h3> </h3>	Creates a third level heading
<h4> </h4>	Creates a fourth level heading
<h5> </h5>	Creates a fifth level heading
<h6> </h6>	Creates a sixth level heading
<a> </a>	Defines a hyperlink
<b> </b>	Defines a bold text
<caption> </caption>	Defines a table caption
<blockquote> </blockquote>	Defines a section quoted from another source
<div> </div>	Defines a section in a document
<dl> </dl>	Defines a definition list

<dt> </dt>	Defines a term in a definition list
<dd> </dd>	Defines a description of an item in a definition list
<img>	Defines an image
<em> </em>	Defines emphasized text
<input> </input>	Defines an input control
<iframe> </iframe>	Defines an inline frame
<object> </object>	Defines an embedded object
<pre> </pre>	Defines a preformatted text
<select> </select>	Defines a drop-down list
<style> </style>	Defines style information for a document
<strong> </strong>	Defines important text
<table> </table>	Defines a table
<tbody> </tbody>	Groups the body content in a table
<th> </th>	Defines a header cell in a table
<td> </td>	Defines a cell in a table
<small> </small>	Defines smaller text
<span> </span>	Defines a section in a document
	Defines a superscripted text
	Defines a subscripted text
<abbr> </abbr>	Defines an acronym or abbreviation
<!--...-->	Creates invisible comment
<button> </button>	Defines a clickable button
<textarea> </textarea>	Defines a multiline input control
<noscript> </noscript>	Defines an alternate content for users that don't support client-side scripts

New Tags in HTML5

New Media Elements

Tag	Function
<video> </video?	Defines video content
<audio> </audio>	Defines sound content
<embed> </embed>	Define a container for interactive content or an external application
<source> </source>	Defines multimedia resources for both audio and video
<track> </track>	Defines text tracks for audio and video

New Elements for Graphics and Forms

<canvas> </canvas>	Used for drawing graphics through scripting
<keygen> </keygen>	Defines a key-pair generator field
<datalist> </datalist>	Specifies a predefined options for input controls
<output> </output>	Defines calculation results

New Structural or Semantic Elements

<article> </article>	Define an article
<section></section>	Creates a section
<aside> </aside>	Defines content related to the page content
<hrgroup> </hrgroup>	Groups a set of h1 to h6 elements
<header> </header>	Defines a header for a section or document and commonly contains the logo, company, and page title

<footer> </footer>	Defines a footer for a section or document
<bdi> </bdi>	isolates a section of a text that might be formatted differently
<nav> </nav>	Defines navigation links
<summary> </summary>	Defines a visible heading for a details element
<details> </details>	Defines other details that users can view or hide
<command> </command>	Defines a command button
<figure> </figure>	Identifies self-contained content
<figcaption> </figcaption>	Defines a caption for a figure element
<meter> </meter>	Defines scalar measurement
<mark> </mark>	Defines highlighted or marked text
<time> </time>	Defines a time or date
<progress> </progress>	Pertains to the status of a task
<ruby> </ruby>	Defines a ruby annotation
<rt> </rt>	Defines a pronunciation or explanation of characters.
<wbr> </wbr>	Defines possible line break
<rp> </rp>	Specifies what to display in browsers that don't support rub annotations

Attributes

An attribute is used to modify an HTML element. It is always placed inside the start tag of the element. Attributes consist of two parts: name and value.

The name is the element's property that you want to define. The value specifies the setting for the property and is usually written inside quotation marks. For example:

<font face= "arial" size="3"> DogHouse </font>

In the above example, the names are 'face' and 'size' while he values are "arial" and "3" respectively.

Attribute name and their values are not case sensitive but the W3C recommends lowercase attributes and values. HTML5 does not require values to be placed inside quotes but the W3c recommends that values be given inside quotes.

Commonly Used Attributes

There are four core attributes that can be used on most HTML elements:

- id
- title
- class
- style

The id attribute

The id attribute can be used to specify a unique identification for an element in an HTML page. For instance, if there are two elements with identical names within the same web page, you may want to use the id attribute to distinguish one from the other.

The title Attribute

The title attribute specifies a title for the element. It is usually displayed as a tool tip when the mouse hovers over the element or when the element is loading. Its behavior, however, depends on the element that uses it.

The class Attribute

The class attribute is most commonly used to associate an element to a class in a style sheet. The value of this attribute may consist of a space-separated list of class names.

The class Attribute

The style attribute lets you define Cascading Style Sheet (CSS) rules on an HTML element.

syntax:

<tagname style="property:value;">

Internationalization Attributes

The following internationalization attributes are available for most XHTML elements:

- dir
- lang
- xml:lang

The dir Attribute

The dir attribute is used to specify the direction of the text in the element's content. In HTML5, the dir attribute can be applied and will validate on any HTML element.

There are three possible values for this global attribute:

ltr   left-to-right text direction (default value)
rtl   right-to-left text direction
auto   allows the browser to determine the text direction based on the content of the element

Syntax:
<element dir="ltr | rtl | auto">

Example:

```
<!DOCTYPE html>
<html dir="ltr">
<head>
<title>Specify Directions</title>
</head>
<body>
This is how the browser renders left-to-right text direction.
</body>
</html>
```

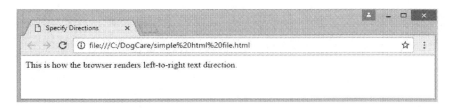

The Lang Attribute

The lang attribute lets you specify the main language of the element's content. It can be used and validated on any HTML5 element.

Syntax:

<element lang="language_code">

The value is any language code such as "en" for English, "de" for German, "es" for Spanish, "fr" for French, and "pt" for Portuguese.

Example:

```
<!DOCTYPE html>
<html lang="es">
<head>
<title>Spanish Language Page</title>
</head>
<body>
This page is using Spanish Language.
</body>
</html>
```

The xml:lang Attribute

The xml:lang attribute is the XHTML replacement for lang attribute. Like the lang attribute, its value should be a country code.

Generic Attributes

The following attributes can be used with many HTML tags:

Attribute	Function	Values
align	aligns tags horizontally	right, left, center
valign	aligns tags vertically within an HTML element.	top, middle, bottom
bgcolor	Sets a background color behind an element	numeric, RGB values, hexidecimal
backgroun	Sets a background image	URL

21

d	behind an element	
id	Specifies an element for use with CSS	User Defined
class	Classifies an element for use with CSS	User Defined
width	Specifies the width of images, table cells, or tables	Numeric
height	Specifies the height of images, table cells, or tables	Numeric
title	Displays title of the elements.	User Defined

Values

Attributes are usually presented in name-value pairs. The value specifies, sets, or defines the properties of an attribute. For example, in the following declaration, the values "Arial" and "24" specifies the attributes face and size respectively. Together, they provide more information about font.

<font face="Arial" size="24"> Dog Care Company </font>

CHAPTER 3: STRUCTURE OF HTML FILES

HTML files have two parts: the head and the body. The data contained in the head parts are enclosed in the tags <head> </head> while the data contained in the body part are enclosed in the tag <body> </body>.

Head Tags

The head tags are placed immediately after the start html tag. It can contain data such as the title of the web page or document, meta information, and scripts.

The <head> element can contain the following elements:

- <title>
- <meta>
- <link>
- <style>
- <base>
- <script>
- <noscript>

HTML5 now validates HTML files even without the <head> tag but a <title> should be included.

Here's an example of an HTML file without a <head> tag:

```
<!DOCTYPE html>
<html>
```

```
<title>Document Title</title>

<body>
<h1>This is a heading</h1>
<p>This is a paragraph.</p>
</body>

</html>
```

Body Tags

The body tags <body> </body> comes immediately after the end head tag and contains everything that should appear on the web page including the text, images, and videos.

Container tags have a start tag and attributes. The body tag is a container tag and has a start tag. Hence, it contains attributes.

These are the attributes for body tags:

text	specifies the text color of the web page
bgcolor	specifies the background color of the web page
background	specifies the background image of the web page
class, style, id	used in CSS
link	specifies the color of hyperlinks in the page
alink	specifies the color of active hyperlinks in the web page
vlink	specifies the color of visited hyperlinks

Headings

Headings are container tags which are used to format heading text using predefined values for colors and sizes. They are used to organize the content of the web page. There are 6 heading tags and they have different effects on the text:

- <h1> </h1>
- <h2> </h2>
- <h3> </h3>
- <h4> </h4>
- <h5> </h5>
- <h6> </h6>

HTML documents may contain a main heading and one or more sub-headings. A font size is assigned to each heading to distinguish it from other headings. The main heading typically has the biggest font size and is defined as <h1>. The next heading is assigned the second biggest font size and is specified as <h2>. This can go on to <h6> which is the smallest heading font. It is assigned to the least important heading.

Headings can be aligned to the right, center, or left of the document.

Here are the attributes of Heading Tags:

Attribute	Meaning
align	Specifies the heading's horizontal alignment
title	Specifies the text that appears each time the mouse hovers over the heading
class, style, id	Used in CSS

Grouping Headings

Headings may be organized or grouped to show the relationship between subheadings, multiple levels, or alternative titles. To do this, you will use the <hgroup> element to group them. You can use two or more of the heading types from h1 to h6.

Using the Header

The header can contain introductory or navigational content of the document. It can include links, search box, or main navigation.

Navigation

Navigation facilitates linking of important groups. A link in the <nav> element may point to data within the page, to other pages, or both. An HTML list can be used as a base for a navigation bar.

Here's a code segment that creates a simple navigation bar from a standard list:

```
<ul>
  <li><a href="cover_image.jpg">Home</a></li>
  <li><a href="spreadsheet.jpg">Status</a></li>
  <li><a href="aboutpage.asp">About</a></li>
  <li><a href="email.asp">Contact</a></li>
</ul>
```

Article

An article refers to a self-contained reusable or distributable composition within the document. It can be a blog post, a forum post, product description, magazine or newspaper article, comment, news story, and similar items. This tag is a new HTML5 feature.

Here's an example:

```
<article>
  <h2>Python</h2>
  <p>Python is an object-oriented general purpose programming
language developed by Guido van Rossum in the late 1980s.</p>
</article>
```

Section

The section element indicates a generic section of a document and usually contains a heading. The section tag, an HTML5 feature, can be used to produce a more creative mark up with options for using the h1 to h6 heading hierarchy.

For example, here is a section which explains what WTO is:

```
<section>
  <h1>WTO</h1>
  <p>The World Trade Organization (WTO) ....</p>
</section>
```

Footer

The footer element is an HTML5 enhancement. It may contain information on authorship, contact, copyright, license agreement, index, sitemap, appendix, internal links, and other similar documents. It can be found in several parts of a document.

Example:

```
<footer>
  <p>Prepared by: Martin Page</p>
<p>Contact details: <a href="mailto:MartPage@yehey.com">
    MartPage@yehey.com</a>.</p>
</footer>
```

Generic Container

The <div>element can be used to wrap a container around a section of content to facilitate effect with Javascript or styling with CSS.

For example, here's a code that will cause a section of the page to be shown in red:

```
<div style="color:red">
  <h1>Main Heading</h1>
  <p>Paragraph.</p>
</div>
```

CHAPTER 4: PARAGRAPHS

Working with Paragraphs

Now that you know how to create your own web page and add functionalities such as title and headings, it's time to learn how to work with paragraphs. HTML's tag for creating a paragraph is <p></p>, a container tag.

Example:

This HTML document consists of three paragraphs and was saved under the file name Dog Breeds.html:

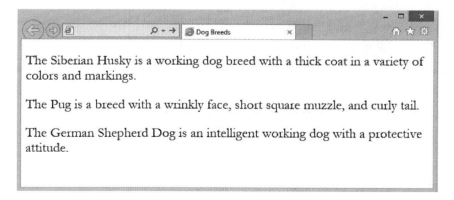

Here's how your web page will look if you view it on your browser:

The Siberian Husky is a working dog breed with a thick coat in a variety of colors and markings.

The Pug is a breed with a wrinkly face, short square muzzle, and curly tail.

The German Shepherd Dog is an intelligent working dog with a protective attitude.

Aligning a Paragraph

To align paragraphs, you will use the paragraph tag pair: <p align=left>, <p align=right>, or the <p align = center>.

Attributes for <p> </p:>

Attribute	Meaning
Align	Specifies the paragraph's horizontal alignment
class, style, ID	Used in CSS

Following is an HTML code with specifications for paragraph alignment:

```
<!DOCTYPE html>
<html>
  <head>
    <title>Dog Breeds</title>
  </head>
    <body>
      <font size="5">
      <h3 align="center">Top Dog Breeds</h3>

    <p align="justify"> A Siberian Husky is a working dog with various coat
markings and colors. The Pug is a breed with a wrinkly face, short square muzzle,
and curly tail. The German Shepherd Dog is an intelligent working dog with a
protective attitude.</p>
        </font>
    <body>
</html>
```

Here's the updated web page:

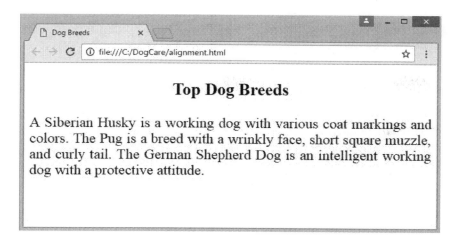

Using Block Quote

The tag pair <blockquote></blockquote> allows you to place quotes in indented form and to shrink them in order to set them apart from the main paragraph.

For example:

```
<!DOCTYPE html>
<html>
  <head>
     <title>Dog Breeds</title>
  </head>
    <body>
       <font size="5">
       <h3 align="center">Top Dog Breeds</h3>
       <p>This is a quotation about dogs.</p>
       <blockquote><font face="Georgia" size="3">
          "This line can be used to insert a quotation about dogs."
       </blockquote>
          <p align="justify"> A Siberian Husky is a working dog in various coat
markings and colors. The Pug is a breed with a wrinkly face, short square muzzle,
and curly tail. The German Shepherd Dog is an intelligent working dog with a
protective attitude.</p>
          </font>
       <body>
</html>
```

Here's how the web page will look at this point:

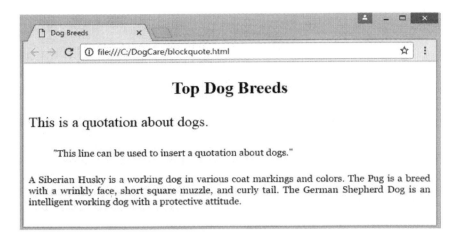

Adding Line Breaks

The <br> tag is used to produce a line break or a new line in text. It is quite useful when you're making files that require specific formatting such as when writing an address or a poem.

```
<!DOCTYPE html>
<html>
  <head>
    <title>Dog Breeds</title>
  </head>
    <body>
      <font size="6" face>
      <h3 align="center">Top Dog Breeds</h3>
              <p align="justify"> A Siberian Husky is a working dog in
      various coat markings and colors. <br> The Pug is a breed with a
      wrinkly face, short square muzzle, and curly tail. <br> The German
      Shepherd Dog is an intelligent working dog with a protective
      attitude.</p>
              </font>
      <body>
</html>
```

Here's a screenshot of the web page that shows how the <br> tags work:

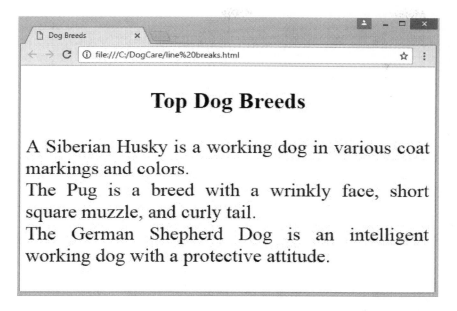

Multiple Line Breaks

The use of multiple <br> tags adds several blank lines to a text. The number of blank lines corresponds to the number of times the tag appears.

For example:

```
<!DOCTYPE html>
<html>
  <head>
    <title>Dog Breeds</title>
  </head>
    <body>
      <font size="5">
```

```
    <h3 align="center">Top Dog Breeds</h3>
    <p>This is a quotation about dogs.</p>
    <blockquote><font face=="Garamond" size="3">
"This line can be used to insert a quotation about dogs."
    </blockquote>
    <p align="justify"> A Siberian Husky is a working dog in various coat
markings and colors. The Pug is a breed with a wrinkly face, short square muzzle,
and curly tail. The German Shepherd Dog is an intelligent working dog with a
protective attitude.</p>

    <br><br><br><br>
Some dogs have temperament that makes them good companions for children.
    </font>
    <body>
</html>
```

Here's what the browser will display:

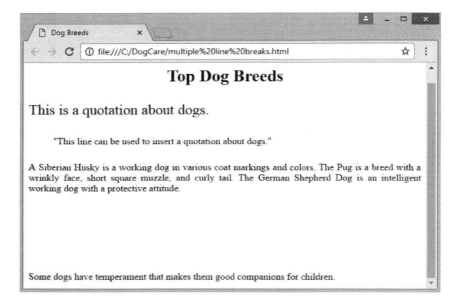

Adding Horizontal Rule

The horizontal rule (hr) tag is used to create a horizontal line that extends up to the full width of the browser. It allows users to add a borderline to a page or underline headlines.

Attributes of the <hr> tag

Attribute	Meaning	Values
align	Identifies the horizontal alignment of the horizontal rule	left, center, right
width	Indicates the horizontal rule's width in pixel or the percent of width displayed	pixels quantity or percent
size	Indicates the size of the horizontal rule in pixels	number of pixels
color	Indicates the color of the horizontal rule	the name of the color or its hexadecimal value
noshade	Tells if the default shading should be removed	none
class, style, id	Used in CSS	

To illustrate, this HTML code is supposed to display a horizontal line over and under the text:

```
<!DOCTYPE html>
<html>
  <head>
     <title>Horizontal Rule</title>
  </head>
    <body>
       <hr>
       <font size="5", face="arial" >
          <p The horizontal rule tag is used to add a borderline across the
          browser window. </p>
          <hr>
          </font>
     <body>
</html>
```

Here's the web page:

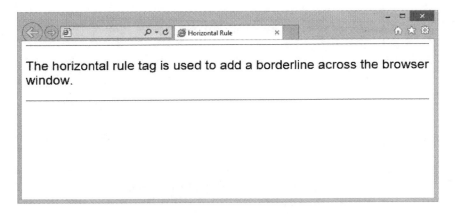

Modifying Horizontal Rules

You can adjust the width, color, or the length of the horizontal line.

For example:

```
<!DOCTYPE html>
<html>
  <head>
     <title>Colorful Lines</title>
  </head>
  </body>
    <br>
    <br>
    <br>
    <hr color="green" width="300" align="right">
    <hr color="blue" width="500" align="center">
    <hr color="red" width="400" align="left">
    <hr noshade size="12">
    <hr color="green" width="500" align="right">
    <hr color="blue" width="400" align="center">
    <hr color="yellow" width="300" align="left">
  </body>
</html>
```

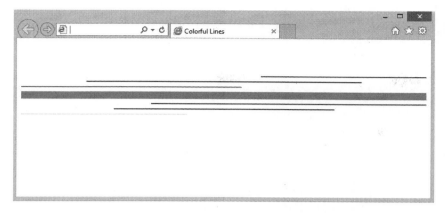

The above illustration showed simple horizontal lines. You can create graphic horizontal rules using GIF images.

Invisible Comments

Web browsers ignore comments and do not display them. Hence, you can use them to store remarks or statements. Comments are indicated by the comment tag <!-- and -->.

Example:

```
<!DOCTYPE html>
<html>
   <head>
      <title>Dog Breeds</title>
   <head>
         <body>
          <!--
             This comment will not be visible on the web page.
          -->
          This page will contain the introduction to the main page.
          </body>
</html>
```

Your web browser will only display the text outside of the comment tags:

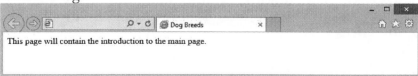

CHAPTER 5: LISTS

HTML provides three ways to specify lists of information:

- <ol>   ordered list
- <ul>   unordered list
- <dl>   definition list

Ordered List

The <ol></ol> tag is a container tag that facilitates the creation of a numbered list or ordered list. The numbering starts at one by default with increments by one. The starting value, however, can be changed using the start attribute. Each item on the list is indicated by the empty tag <li>.

Attributes for the <ol></ol> tag:

Attribute	Meaning	Values
type	Specifies the type of numbering	a, A, 1, i, I
start	Specifies the starting value or number in the list	any number

The type attribute is used to specify the preferred type of numbering for the list. The default type is the number type but there are five options to choose from:

<ol type="1">   default case
<ol type="a">   letters - lowercases
<ol type="A">   letters - uppercase
<ol type="i">   Roman Numerals – lowercase
<ol type="I">   Roman Numerals- uppercase

The start attribute is used to indicate the starting point for the numbering you may require. Here are some code examples:

<ol type="1" start="5">	Numerals start with 5.
<ol type="I" start="5">	Roman numerals start with V.
<ol type="i" start="5">	Roman numerals start with v.
<ol type="a" start="5">	Letters starts with e.
<ol type="A" start="5">	Letters starts with E.

Example:

```
<!DOCTYPE html>
<html>
  <head>
    <title>Various Lists</title>
  <body>
    <h3>Types of Sentences</h3>
    <ol>
        <li>Declarative sentence
        <li>Interrogative sentence
        <li>Imperative sentence
        <li>Exclamatory sentence
    </ol>
    <h3>Primary Colors</h3>
    <ol type="I">
        <li>red
        <li>blue
        <li>yellow
    </ol>
    <h3>Vowels</h3>
    <ol type="A" start ="4">
        <li>a
        <li>b
        <li>c
    </ol>
  </body>
</html>
```

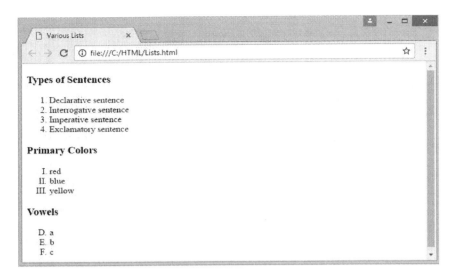

Unordered List

An unordered list refers to a collection of related items with no sequence or order. It is a bulleted list which is created with the <ul> tag.

Attribute	Meaning	Values
type	Specifies the type of bullet to be used	disc, square, circle

Disc refers to the filled round bullets:
<ul style="list-style-type: disc">

Square signifies square bullets:
<ul style="list-style-type: square">

Circle refers to the unfilled, circular bullets:
<ul style="list-style-type: circle">

Example:

```
<!DOCTYPE html>
<html>
```

```
<head>
  <title>Various Lists</title>
<body>
  <h3>Planets</h3>
  <ul style="list-style-type: disc">
      <li>Mars</li>
      <li>Mercury</li>
      <li>Venus </li>
      <li>Earth </li>
  </ul>
  <body>
<html>
```

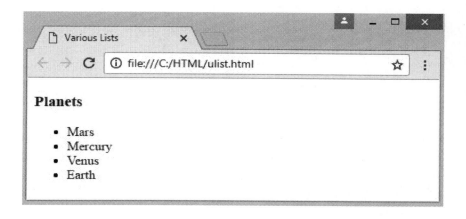

Definition List

HTML support the Definition List, a type of list in which entries are listed alphabetically. This is used to present a list of terms and their definition or a glossary in your web page.

Definition List uses the following tags:

<dl>   Definition List start tag
<dt>   A term
<dd>   Definition of the term

</dl> Definition List end tag

Example:

```
<!DOCTYPE html>
<html>
  <head>
    <title>Dog Foods</title>
  </head>
  <body>
    <h3>Types of Dog Foods</h3>
    <dl>
      <dt>Dry Foods
        <dd>Dry foods are low moisture foods that include
            flakefoods, biscuits, or extruded foods. They have
            high protein content and often contain meat as
            ingredient.
      <dt>Wet Foods
        <dd>Wet foods have high moisture content, are cooked
            in high temperature, and canned under high
            pressure.
      <dt>Semi-Moist Foods
        <dd>Semi-moist foods have chewy texture and are sold
            in soft pellets.
    </dl>
  </body>
<html>
```

This is how the browser will display the web page:

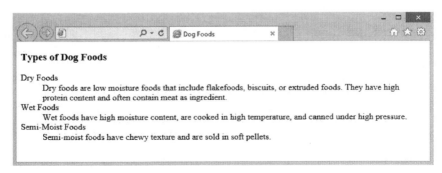

42

Preformatting Text

Preformatted text is more frequently used for formatting computer code or guitar tab in text files. HTML allows preformatting using the tag pair <pre> </pre>.

Example:

```
<!DOCTYPE html>
<html>
  <head>
    <title>Computer Software</title>
  </head>
    <body>
      <font size="5" face="arial">
      This will list items in columns:
    <pre>
          Word            Excel            Visio
            Powerpoint    Access           Outlook
    </pre>
    </body>
</html>
```

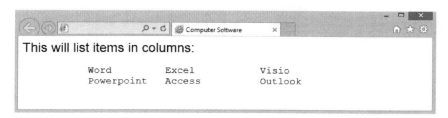

Nesting Tags

Nesting tags refer to the practice of putting a tag within a tag. The following line of code will display a given text in boldface (b) and italics (i):

<b><i> text</i></b>

Notice that nested tags are closed in the reverse order that they were opened.

To illustrate, here's a code that uses nested tags to show the different styling elements for text:

```
<head>
    <title>Nested tags</title>
</head>
<body>
    This displays text in <b><i> boldface and italics</i></b>.
    <br><br>
    This displays <u><em>underlined and emphasized </em></u> text.
    <br><br>
    This displays <u>underlined</u> text in <u> <b> <i> boldface and
    italics </i> </b> <u>.
<body>
```

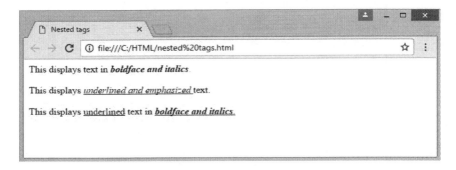

Nesting Lists

Nesting list is the practice of placing lists under another list. For example, you can place an ordered list inside an unordered list.

```
<!DOCTYPE html>
<html>
    <head>
        <title>Nested Lists</title>
    </head>
    <body>
        <h3>Colors</h3>
        <ol>
```

44

```
<li>Primary
  <ul>
      <li>Red
        <li>Blue
        <li>Yellow
  </ul>
 <li>Secondary
      <ul>
        <li>Green
        <li>Orange
         <li>Violet
      </ul>
 <li>Terciary
      <ul>
          <li>Red Violet
           <li>Red Orange
          <li>Blue Violet
          <li>Blue Green
          <li>Yellow Green
          <li>Yellow Orange
      <ul>
</ol>
 </body>
</html>
```

CHAPTER 6: STYLING TEXT

HTML formatting elements are used to style special types of text.

The following table shows the different elements you can use for styling text:

\<b\>	Defines boldface text
\<strong\>	Defines prominent text
\<mark\>	Used to highlight or mark text
\<i\>	Defines italicized text
\<em\>	Used to emphasize text
\<small\>	Defines smaller text
\<ins\>	Used to add text
\<del\>	Used to add strikethrough style
\<sup\>	Defines superscripts
\<sub\>	Defines subscripts

HTML \<b\>\</b\> Element

The \<b\>\</b\> element indicates a regular bold text with no added prominence.

You can style body text in boldface by placing it inside the \<b\>\</b\> tag. The following code demonstrates how you can easily specify an entire paragraph to be displayed in boldface:

```
<body>
<p>This paragraph uses normal text.</p>
<p><b>This paragraph shows boldface text.</b></p>
</body>
```

46

HTML <strong></strong> Element

The HTML <strong></strong> element specifies text with bigger semantic significance. Your browser, however, will display the text in boldface.

For example:

```
<p>This paragraph uses boldface text.</p>
<p><strong>This paragraph uses strong text. </strong></p>
```

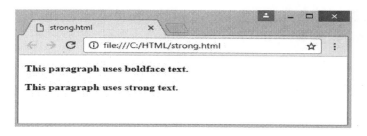

HTML <mark></mark> Element

The <mark></mark> element specifies highlighted or marked text.

Example:

```
<body>
<h2>Great Publishers will release <mark>ten programming
books</mark> this weekend.</h2>
</body>
```

The HTML <i></i> and <em></em> Elements

The <i></i> element defines regular italic text with no added prominence. On the other hand, the <em></em> element specifies text with greater semantic importance. Your browser, however, will display both text styles in italics.

To demonstrate, here's a code showing italicized and emphasized text:

```
<p><i>This paragraph shows italicized text.<i></p>
<p><em>This paragraph shows emphasized text.</em></p>
```

This is how the browser implements the code. Notice that there's no difference between the emphasized and italicized text when it comes to output:

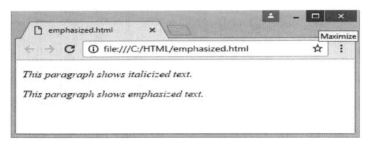

HTML <small></small> Element

The <small></small> tags defines text in smaller fonts than normal.

For example:

```
<body>
<p>This paragraph uses the <small>small formatting</small> style.</p>
```

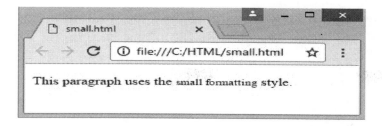

HTML <del></del> Element

The <del></del> element is used to output deleted or removed text with strikethrough effects.

Example:

<p>My pet is a smart <del>tiger</del> cat.</p>

HTML <ins></ins> Element

The <ins></ins> element specifies inserted/added text.

<p>My pet<ins>cat</ins> is called Snaky.</p>

HTML Element

The element specifies subscripted text.

The following code snippet demonstrates how you can use this element to style text with subscripts in HTML:

```
<p>You're reading a <sub>subscript</sub>.</p>
```

HTML Element

The element specifies superscripted text.

This code demonstrates how to style text with superscripts in HTML:

```
<body>
You're seeing an example of <sup>superscript </sup>.</p>
</body>
```

CHAPTER 7: USING COLORS

Colors help provide a specific look and feel to your site. You can use the <body> tag to specify page color or the bg color attribute to set the color for each tag.

The <body> tag

The <body> tag has some attributes that can be used for setting colors:

bgcolor	used to set a color for the page background
text	used to set a color for the text
alink	used to set a color for active or specified links
link	used to manage the color of a linked text
vlink	used to set a color for a linked text that had been clicked on or visited

Color Setting Methods

These three methods are used to set the colors in your web pages:

Color names	used when directly specifying color names such as green, red, or blue
Hex codes	a six-digit code that stands for the amount of blue, green, or red that will constitute a desired color
RGV Value	this value uses the rgb property for color setting

Color Names

You can define a specific color name when setting the color of the text or the background. While there are 16 color names that will

51

pass an HTML validator, major browsers support more than 200 color names.

Here are the 16 HTML colors:

Hex Value	Name	Color
#ffff00	yellow	
#008080	teal	
#c0c0c0	silver	
#800080	purple	
#ff0000	red	
#000080	navy	
#808000	olive	
#00ff00	lime	
#800000	maroon	
#808080	gray	
#008000	green	
#000000	black	
#ff00ff	fuchsia	
#0000ff	blue	
#00ffff	aqua	
#ffffff	white	

Hex Codes

A hex code or hexadecimal is a 6-digit representation of the colors red (first two digits), green (middle two digits), and blue (last two digits). A pound or hash # sign precedes each hex code.

RGB Values

This method uses the rgb property to specify the color value. The rgb property has three values: red, green, and blue. The value can be a percentage or an integer from zero to 255. Currently, no browser support the rgb() color property so it is not a recommended method.

Following are examples of colors that use the rgb values:

rgb(0,0,0)	
rgb(0,0,255)	
rgb(0,255,0)	
rgb(0,255,255)	
rgb(192,192,192)	
rgb(255,0,0)	
rgb(255,0,255)	
rgb(255,255,0)	
rgb(255,255,255)	

CHAPTER 8: BACKGROUND AND IMAGES

While the default webpage background is white, HTML allows you to decorate your page background in two ways:

- Background with Color(s)
- Background with Images

Background with Colors

You can change the background color of your webpage using the bgcolor attribute. Here is the syntax to use this attribute with other HTML tags:

<tagname bgcolor="value">

The value pertains to the color that you want to use and may be specified using any of these three formats:

Format 1: Using the color name
<body bgcolor= "green" >

Format 2: Using the hex value
<body bgcolor="#ff0000" >

Format 3: Use the RGB color value
<body bgcolor="rgb(0,0,120)" >

Example:

<!DOCTYPE html>
<html>

```
<head>
  <title>HTML Background Colors</title>
</head>
<body>
<!--Use a color name to designate background color -->
    <table bgcolor="blue" width="100%">
    <tr><td>
      A webpage can have a blue background.
    </td></tr>
    </table>
<!--Use the hex value to specify background color-->
    <table bgcolor="#ff0000">
    <tr><td>
      This section uses a red background.
    </td></tr>
    </table>
<!--Use the RGB value to specify background color-->
    <table bgcolor="rgb(255,255,0)">
    <tr><td>
      This section uses a yellow background.
    </td></tr>
    </table>
  </body>
</html>
```

This is how the browser will likely display the web page:

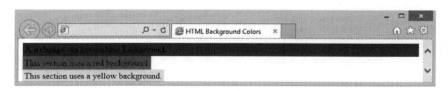

Background with Images

The background attribute has been deprecated in HTML5 and users are advised to use the Styling Sheets for setting the background.

Working with Images

Images make web pages more attractive and help site owners depict complex concepts in a simpler way.

Preparing the Image

You can create an image using image editing programs such as Adobe Photoshop or MS Paint. You must save the image in a JPEG or PNG format and compress the file for faster loading time. You can choose to save the file for web use in order to reduce image size.

HTML supports the following file types or image formats:

JPEG or JPG (Joint Photographic Experts Group)

This format supports a million colors and is the most commonly used one. The filename's extension is either jpeg or jpg.

GIF (Compuserve Graphics Interchange Format)

The GIF format supports up to 256 colors with a filename extension of gif. It is a commonly used format that can be animated.

PNG (Portable Network Graphics)

The PNG format supports a million colors and uses the filename extension png.

BMP (Bitmap)

The BMP format supports a million colors and has the filename extension of bmp. This file provides the best quality because it is not compressed. The cost, however, is its large image size.

Inserting an Image

The <img> tag is used to add images to the web pages while the src= attribute is used to specify the name and location of the image. The <img> is an empty tag. Hence, it has no closing tag and can only contain attribute(s).

<img> Attributes

Attribute	Meaning
src	Specifies the image to be used
alt	Indicates the alternate text that will appear when the mouse hovers over the image or when the image cannot be displayed
height	Specifies the image height in pixels. If not specified, the image will be scaled to fit.
width	Specifies the image width in pixels. If not specified, the image will be scaled to fit.
usemap	Defines an image as a client-side image map
ismap	Defines an image as a server-side image map

To insert the image, you will use the <img> tag. To display the image or the alternate text, you will use the attributes src= and alt=.

The syntax is:

<img src="image filename" alt="alternate text">

Example:

```
<!DOCTYPE html>
<html>
  <head>
    <title>Funny Dogs</title>
  </head>
    <body>
      <img src="c/laughingdogs.jpeg" alt="funny dogs"
      width="200" height="250"/><br>
        Happy Dogs
    </body>
</html>
```

HTML5 does not support <hspace>, <vpace> <hspace>, <border>, and <align> tags and you must use CSS to set the horizontal space, vertical space, image border, and alignment of the image.

CHAPTER 9: TABLES

Tables let you organize and arrange data like text, images, or links into rows and columns. This feature allows you to divide the page into different sections that can accommodate navigation links, headers, and footers.

Creating a Table

HTML tables are created with the <table> tag. The <tr> tag is used to define table rows while the <td> is used to define data cells within the row.

Example:

```html
<!DOCTYPE html>
<html>
<head>
<title>Company Officials</title>
</head>
<body>
<caption>Corporate Heads</caption>
<table border="1" bordercolor="blue"
    <tr bgcolor="silver">
        <th></th>
    </tr>
    <tr>
        <th align="center" width="200px">Name</th>
        <th align="center" width="200px">Position</th>
        <th align="center" width="200px">Department</th>
    </tr>
    <tr>
        <td align="center"> Jack Mccalister</td>
        <td align="center">CEO</td>
        <td align="center">Executive</td>
    </tr>
    <tr>
        <td align="center"> Jane March</td>
        <td align="center">President</td>
        <td align="center">Executive</td>
    </tr>
    <tr>
        <td align="center"> Shane Dans</td>
        <td align="center">IT Manager</td>
        <td align="center">Data Processing</td>
    </td>
</table>
</body>
</html>
```

Your web browser will display the table below:

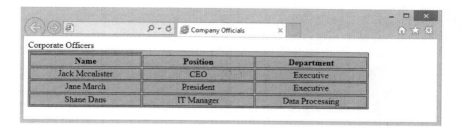

Modifying a Table

There are different ways to change the appearance of a table. You can set its background color or image, change the color and thickness of the border, or set the distance between the border and the cell content. These are carried out using the table's attributes.

Here are the attributes of HTML tables:

Attribute	Meaning	Values
align	Indicates the table's horizontal alignment	left, center, right
background	Indicates the table's background image	filename with path
bgcolor	Indicates the table's background color	color's name or hex value
border	Indicates the border's thickness in pixels	number of pixels
bordercolor	Indicates the border's color	color name or hex value
width	Indicates the table's width in pixels or percentage of the width displayed by the web browser	number of pixels or percentage of the width displayed
cellpadding	Indicates the distance between cell content and the borders around it in pixels	number of pixels
cellspacing	Indicates the distance between the cells in pixel	number of pixels

Setting the Background

There are two ways to set the background of the table:

Using bgcolor attribute

This attribute will allow you to set back background color for the entire table or for one table cell.

Using background attribute

This attribute will allow you to set the background image for one cell or the entire table.

Cellpadding and Cellspacing Attributes

The attributes cellspacing and cellpadding lets you adjust the white space in your table cells. The cellpadding attribute tells the distance between the cell content and cell borders inside the cell. The cellspacing attribute indicates the border's width.

Table Header, Body, and Footer

Tables may be divided into three sections: the head, the body, and the foot. The body is the principal data holder of the table while the headers and footers can be compared to the headers and footers found in a word processing document that displays the same value for each page.

The following are the three elements used to separate the body, the header, and the footer of a table:

<thead>   used to create a separate header
<tbody>   indicates the main body
<tfoot>   creates a separate footer

A table may have one or more <tbody> elements to denote the groups or pages of data but the <thead> and <tfoot> must appear before it.

For example, to change or set the border thickness, border color, width, cell spacing, and cell padding of the above table example:

```
<!DOCTYPE html>
<html>
<head>
<title>Company Officials</title>
</head>
<body>
 <table align="center" border="3" bordercolor="green"
width="600"  cellpadding="5"  cellspacing="7">
    <caption><h3>Corporate Heads</h3></caption>
    <tr>
        <td><b>Name</b></td>
        <td><b>Position</b></td>
        <td><b>Department</b></td>
    </tr>
    <tr>
        <td>Jack Mccalister</td>
        <td>CEO</td>
        <td>Executive</td>
    </tr>
     <tr>
         <td>Jane March</td>
        <td>President</td>
        <td>Executive</td>
    </tr>
    <tr>
         <td> Shane Dans</td>
        <td>IT Manager</td>
        <td>Data Processing</td>
      </td>
</table>
</body>
</html>
```

Here's the modified table:

Notice that the table headings were displayed in bold fonts and the caption 'Corporate Heads' was center aligned and shown in bold face.

Modifying Table Rows

You can change a specific row's <tr></tr> appearance through the row's attributes.

Here are the attributes for <tr></tr>:

Attribute	Meaning	Values
align	Specifies the horizontal alignment of a row's content	left, center, right
valign	Specifies the vertical alignment of a row's content	top, middle, bottom
bgcolor	Specifies the row's background color	color name or hex value
height	Specifies the row height in pixels	number or pixels

To illustrate, you can change the background color and alignment of the above table's header row with the following code:

```
<!DOCTYPE html>
<html>
<head>
<title>Company Officials</title>
</head>
```

```
<body>
 <table align="center" border="3" bordercolor="green"
width="600" cellpadding="5" cellspacing="7">
    <caption><h3>Corporate Heads</h3></caption>
    <tr height=35" bgcolor="lime", align="center">
        <td><b>Name</b></td>
        <td><b>Position</b></td>
        <td><b>Department</b></td>
    </tr>
    <tr>
        <td>Jack Mccalister</td>
        <td>CEO</td>
        <td>Executive</td>
    </tr>
    <tr>
<td>Jane March</td>
        <td>President</td>
        <td>Executive</td>
    </tr>
    <tr>
<td> Shane Dans</td>
        <td>IT Manager</td>
        <td>Data Processing</td>
    </td>
</table>
</body>
</html>
```

This is how the web browser will display the modified table:

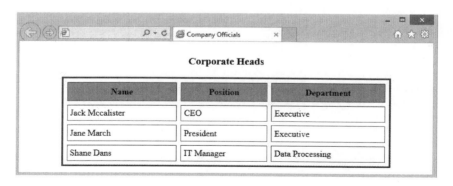

Modifying Table Data

You can change the appearance of <td></td> data on each cell through their attributes.

Here are the <td></td> attributes:

Attribute	Meaning
bgcolor	Specifies the row's background color
background	Defines the cell's background image
align	Specifies the horizontal alignment of the cell content
valign	Specifies the vertical alignment of the cell content
nowrap	Prevents word wrapping in a cell
height	Indicates the cell's height in pixels
width	Indicates the table's width in pixels or percent of the table's width
rowspan	Merges several rows
colspan	Merges several cells

For example, the following code modifies the background color and alignment of the above table's first column:

```
<head>
<title>Company Officials</title>
</head>
<body>
 <table align="center" border="3" bordercolor="green"
width="600" cellpadding="5" cellspacing="7">
   <caption><h3>Corporate Heads</h3></caption>
   <tr height=35" bgcolor="lime", align="center">
     <th><b>Name</b></th>
     <th><b>Position</b></th>
     <th><b>Department</b></th>
   </tr>
   <tr>
     <td align="center" bgcolor="yellow">Jack Mccalister</td>
     <td>CEO</td>
     <td>Executive</td>
   </tr>
```

```
<tr>
   <td align="center" bgcolor="yellow">Jane March</td>
   <td>President</td>
   <td>Executive</td>
</tr>
<tr>
<td align="center" > bgcolor="yellow">Shane Dans</td>
   <td>IT Manager</td>
   <td>Data Processing</td>
</td>
</table>
</body>
</html>
```

Here's the modified table showing yellow as the background color for the first column:

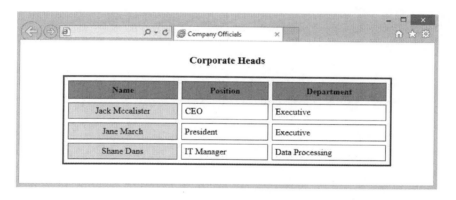

Merging Cells

Merging Cells Horizontally

You can merge cells in the same row with the use of the colspan attribute of <th></th> and <td></td>.

Example:

```
<!DOCTYPE html>
<html>
```

```
<head>
  <title>Simple Table</title>
</head>
<body>
  <table align= "center" border="3" width="600">
    <tr>
      <td colspan="3">Science</td>
    </tr>
    <tr>
      <td>Botany</td>
      <td>Zoology</td>
      <td>Bacteriology</td>
    </tr>
    <tr>
      <td>Entomology</td>
      <td>Ornitology</td>
      <td>Ecology</td>
    </tr>
  </table>
</body>
</html>
```

The table below shows that the first three columns on the first row were merged into one cell using the colspan= attribute:

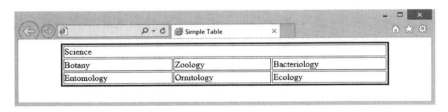

Merging Cells Vertically

Cells in adjacent rows can be merged with the use of the rowspan attribute of <th></th> and <td></td>.

Example:

```
<!DOCTYPE html>
<html>
  <head>
    <title>Simple Table</title>
```

68

```
</head>
<body>
  <table align= "center" border="3" width="600">
    <tr>
        <td rowspan="3">Science</td>
        <td colspan="2">Biology</td>
    </tr>
    <tr>
        <td>Zoology </td>
        <td>Botany<td>
    </tr>
      <tr>
        <td>Bacteriology</td>
        <td>Entomology</td>
    </table>
  </body>
</html>
```

This is how the table will appear on the browser:

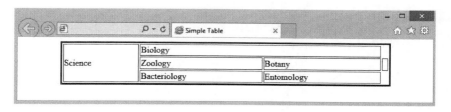

The attribute rowspan= merged the three adjacent rows into one cell while colspan= merged two adjacent cells in the same row.

Merging Cells Vertically and Horizontally

Merged cells on one row can be merged with cells on the adjacent rows by using the colspan= and rowspan= together.

Example:

```
<head>
  <title>Simple Table</title>
</head>
<body>
  <table align="center" border="2" width="600">
    <tr>
```

```
        <td>R1A</td>
          <td colspan="2" rowspan="2">Merged Rows 1&2 B&C</td>
      </tr>
      <tr>
        <td>R2A</td>
      </tr>
      <tr>
        <td>R3A</td>
        <td>R3B</td>
        <td>R3C</td>
      </tr>
    </table>
</body>
```

The table below shows the merged rows 1 and 2 and cells B and C:

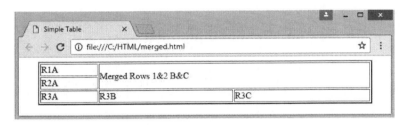

Nesting Tables

HTML lets you place a table inside another table. This technique helps enhance the structure and layout of the webpage.

Example:

```
<!DOCTYPE html>
<html>
  <head>
    <title>HTML Tables</title>
  </head>
    <body>
      <table border="1" width="100%">
    <tr>
        <td width="30%" valign="center">
          <h3 align="center">LINKS</h3>
```

70

```
<ul>
     <li><a href="home.html">Home</a>
     <li><a href="novels.html">Novels</a>
        <li><a href="songs.html">Songs</a>
        <li><a href="poems.html">Poems</a>
        <li><a href="messages.html">Messages</a>
   <ul>
</td>
<td>
          <table align="center" border="3"        bordercolor="green"
          width="600" cellpadding="5" cellspacing="7">
       <caption><h3>CorporateHeads</h3></caption>
        <tr>
                <th>Name</th>
                <th>Position</th>
                <th>Department</th>
        </tr>
        <tr>
                <td>Jack Mccalister</td>
                <td>CEO</td>
                <td>Executive</td>
        </tr>
        <tr>
                <td>Jane March</td>
        <td>President</td>
        <td>Executive</td>
        </tr>
        <tr>
                <td>Shane Dans</td>
        <td>IT Manager</td>
        <td>Data Processing</td>
        </tr>
   </table>
 </body>
</html>
```

The web browser will show the following nested table:

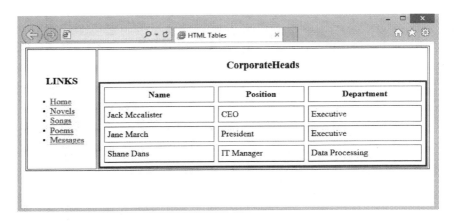

Adding Image

You can easily add an image to a cell with the tag <td><img src="...">.

Example:

```
<!DOCTYPE html>
<html>
 <head>
<title>Dog Breeds</title>
</head>
<body>
<caption>Dog Breeds</caption>
<table border="2" bordercolor= ="red" bgcolor="green">
  <tr bgcolor="yellow">
    <th></th>
  </tr>
  <tr>
    <td align="center" width="200px">Pug</td>
    <td align="center" width="200px">Poodle</td>
    <td align="center" width="200px">Shi Tzu</td>
  </tr>
  <tr>
      <td><img src="e\pug.jpeg" width="200">  height="200"> </td>
      <td align="center">Image Not Available</td>
      <td align="center">Image Not Available</td>
  </tr>
</table>
</body>
</html>
```

72

This is how the above table will appear on the web browser:

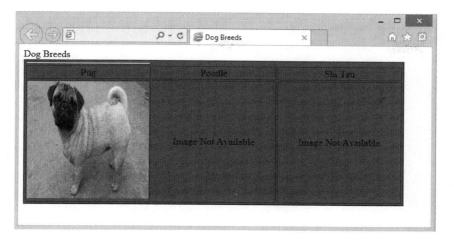

73

CHAPTER 10: HYPERLINKS

A website usually consists of multiple web pages. Hyperlink is the reference link that lets users navigate through the different pages of a website or to a webpage of another website. An underlined colored text or an image may be used to represent the link.

Types of Hyperlink

Absolute link	Links to a page on a different site
Relative link	Links to a page on the same site
Anchor link	Links to a different section on the same web page or website

Linking a Page to Another File or Web Page

Anchors allow web users to navigate to another file or web page. When clicked, hyperlinks enable viewers to go to the specified web page. Anchors are created using the container tag <a></a> called anchor tags and by setting the value of the href attribute to the target page.

Example:

<a href="www.google.com">Google</a>

Attributes of <a></a>

Attribute	Meaning
href	Specifies the anchor target
target	Indicates what the web browser will do when the hyperlink is clicked
name	Assigns a name to the anchor that defines an internal bookmark

Target Attribute

The target attribute indicates the location where the linked document is opened. It can have the following values:

blank   the value of the target url or href attribute will be opened in a different tab or window

_self   the value of the target url or href attribute will be opened in the same frame

_top   the value of the target url or the href attribute will be opened in the full body of the window

_parent   the value of the target url or the href attribute will be opened in the parent frame

Targetframe   the value of the linked document is opened in a named targetframe

Creating an Email Link

An email link allows your website mails to be sent to your default mail client or MS Outlook Express. You can make an email hyperlink by setting the 'href' attribute to 'mail to' and providing the email address.

Example:

<a href=mailto:cars@yahoo.com>Please send us an email</a>

CHAPTER 11: FORMS

HTML forms facilitate the collection of data from site visitors or viewers. You may want, for instance, to collect information such as name, email address, or credit card number during user registration.

A form takes input from the site user and posts it to a backend application such as CGI, PHP script, or ASP script which will then process the form. It can have sections such as fields, text boxes, or text fields.

There are several ways for users to key in the required information:

- Drop down menus
- Textboxes
- Check boxes
- Radio buttons
- Text areas
- Submit buttons
- Password boxes
- Reset or clear buttons

An HTML form has the following attributes:

Attribute	Meaning	Values
action	Specifies where the information will be submitted	Filename
method	Specifies the method of submission	post, get

The action attribute is used to indicate where the information will be submitted or the backend script that will process the data. The method attribute indicates how the information will be submitted. The get method adds the data into the URL and is used primarily for retrieving data while the post method is used to save or update data.

Creating a Form

The container tag form></form> is used to create a form.

Example:

```
<!DOCTYPE html>
<html>
  <head>
    <title>HTML Forms</title>
  </head>
  <body>
  <h2>Member Information Form</h2>
        <form action="process.html" method="post">
        Username: <input name="textbox1" types="text">
        <br></br>
        Password: <input name="password1" type="password">
        <br></br>
        <input type="radio" name="radio1" checked>Male<br>
 <input type="radio" name="radio1" >Female<br>
        <br>
<input type="checkbox" name="checkboxEG"> Electronics and Gadgets<br>
<input    type="checkbox"    name="checkboxFH">    Furniture    and
Household<br>
<input type="checkbox" name="checkboxPA"> Paints and Accessories <br>
<br>
Select city:<br>
<select name="select1" size="1">
<option value="newyorkcity"> New York City</option>
<option value="sanfrancisco"> San Francisco </option>
<option value="losangeles"> Los Angeles </option>
</select><br>
<br>
Tell us about yourself:<br>
<textarea name="tellmore" rows="5" cols="25"
wrap= "hard">Please tell us more about yourself.
        </textarea><br><br>
        <input type="submit"    value="Submit"
<input type="reset"    value="Clear"
        </form>
  </body>
```

</html>

The above code will produce the following HTML form:

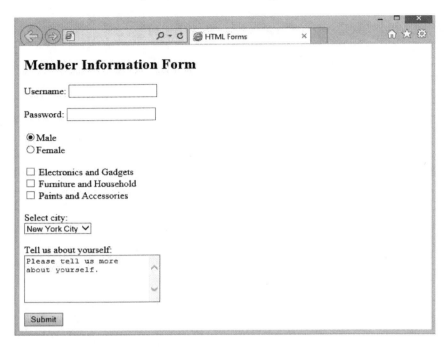

Notice how the radio button has the checked field, Male, as the default field.

New HTML5 Elements

HTML5 has introduced new form elements that can help web designers provide more information and improve page functionality.

Attribute	Function
progress	shows completion level of a task

The progress attribute displays the progress value of a task.

Example:

78

```
<progress value="25" max="100"></progress>
```

Attribute	Function
meter	represents a scalar measurement

The meter attribute represents a scalar measurement within a known range.

Example:

```
<meter value="2" min="0" max="10">2 out of 10</meter><br>
<meter value="0.5">50%</meter>
```

Attribute	Function
datalist	defines a list of pre-defined options

The datalist attribute indicates a list of pre-defined options or provides an autocomplete option on the input element.

Example:

```
<datalist id="cities"
<option value="New York"
</datalist>
```

Attribute	Function
keygen	Defines a key-pair generator field

The keygen attribute defines a key-pair generator that can be used with forms.

This code screenshot demonstrates how you can set the key-pair generator:

```
<form action="demo_keygen.asp"
method="get">
  Username: <input type="text"
name="user_name">
  Encryption: <keygen name="security">
  <input type="submit"></form>
```

Attribute	Function
Output	performs and displays the calculation results

The output attribute performs calculation and displays the result in an output element.

Example:

```
<form oninput="x.value=parseInt(a.val
ue)+parseInt(b.value)">0
  <input type="range" id="a" value="5
0">100

+<input type="number" id="b" value=
"50">
        =<output name="x" for="a
b"></output></form>
```

The Input Element

The form's input element as defined by the <input> empty tag is used to make textboxes, radio buttons, password boxes, submit buttons, and reset buttons depending on the value given for the type attribute. Hence, it can be a text, radio, password, submit, and reset respectively.

Attributes for <input>

Attribute	Function	Values
name	Assigns name to an input field	text without spaces
type	Specifies the type of input field	text, checkbox, radio, password, submit, reset
size	Specifies the size of the input field	number
value	Specifies the initial value of the input field	text
checked	Indicates that a default input field must be selected/checked when the page loads	none

The checked attribute requires no value. It is a Boolean attribute that can be used with the checkbox and radio input types.

Input Types:

Input Type	Function
text	creates a text input field

Creating a Textbox

A textbox is a single line input box. It is commonly used for username input and for entering other one-line text such as names and email address.

Example:

```
<!DOCTYPE html>
<html>
  <body>
  <form action="action_page.php">
  Name:<br>
  <input type="text" name="name">
  <br>
  Email Address:<br>
  <input type="text" name="emailadd">
  <br><br>
  <input type="submit">
  </form>
  </body>
</html>
```

This is how the browser will display the text box:

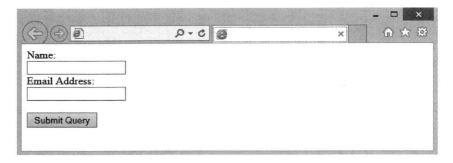

Large Text Areas

HTML allows you to create a text field that can span multiple rows and columns. If you want your readers to share their opinions, recommendations, feedback, requests, or other messages on your website, you need a large text area to accommodate them.

Text areas are made using the container tag <textarea></textarea>. The content inside the tag are shown on the text area.

Example:

82

```
<!DOCTYPE html>
<html>
  <head>
    <title>Home Center</title>
  </head>
    <body>
      <form form action="action_page.php" method="post">
      <h3>Customer Review Form</h3>
      <hr align="left" />
      <h5>Name<input type="text" /></font></p></h5>
      <p>Please help us serve you better by writing a review.<br>
      </font>
      <textarea name="review" rows=="12" cols="40">
      </textarea></p>
      </form>
    </body>
</html>
```

This is how your browser may display the form:

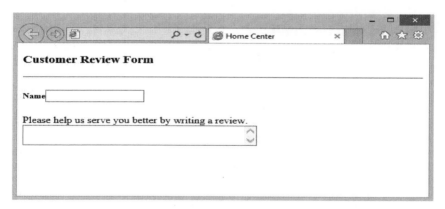

Attributes for <textarea></textarea>

Attribute	Function	Values
name	Assigns a name to the text area	text (with no spaces)
cols	Specifies the width of the text area or the number of columns	number
rows	Specifies the height of the text area or the number of rows	number
wrap	Indicates the type of word wrapping	hard, soft, off
maxlength	Specifies the maximum number of characters allowed in the text area	number
form	Specifies the form(s) that the text area belongs to	form_id
required	Indicates that a text area must be filled out	required
autofocus	Specifies a text area that should automatically get the focus when the page loads	autofocus

Hard word wrapping wraps the text in the text area and upon submission while soft word wrapping only wraps the text in the text area. You can key in the value 'off' to remove word wrapping.

Creating Radio Buttons

Radio buttons provide users a few options where only one can be selected.

```
<!DOCTYPE html>
<html>
 <body>
  <form action="action_page.php">
    <h3>Customer Purchase Information</h3>
    <input type="radio" name="books" value="MSE" checked>  Microsoft
Excel<br>
    <input type="radio" name="books" value="MSW"> Microsoft  Word<br>
    <input type="radio" name="books" value="PP"> Microsoft  PowerPoint
<br><br>
    <input type="submit">
  </form>
  </body>
</html>
```

This is how the web browser will display the radio buttons:

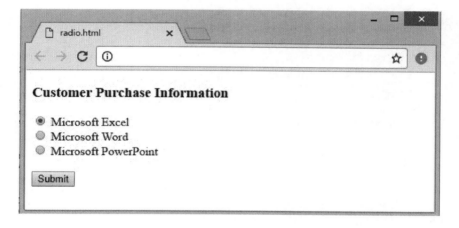

Creating Check Boxes

Check boxes provide user several options and allow none, one, or many to be selected. The 'checked' attribute may be used to indicate the default option.

Example:

```
<!DOCTYPE html>
<html>
 <body>
 <form action="action_page.php">
 <h3>Customer Purchase Form</h3>
 <hr align="left" />
 <p>Please check the products(s) you have purchased in the past   3
years:<br></br>
  <input type="checkbox" name="software" value="cross">
  MS Excel</font></p>
  <input type="checkbox" name="software" value="cross">
  MS Word</font></p>
  <input type="checkbox" name="software" value="cross">
  MS Powerpoint</font></p>
  </form>
  </body>
</html>
```

The above code will create the following form:

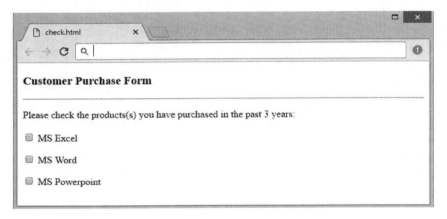

Creating Drop-down Menus

Drop-down menus offer a list of choices where only one can be selected. They are created using the tag <select></select>.

Attributes for <select></select>

Attribute	Function	Values
name	Assigns a name to the dropdown menu	any text without space
size	Indicates the number of visible lines/items	number

Example:

```
<!DOCTYPE html>
<html>
  <head>
    <title>Technical Training</title>
  </head>
    <body>
      <caption>Technical Courses</caption>
      <hr width="25%" align="left"/>
      <form action="action_page.php" method="post">
      <h3>Student Application Form</h3>
      <p>Please select a course:
      <select name="coursechoice" size="2"
      <option>Welding</option>
      <option>Automotive Mechanics</option>
      <option>Industrial Sewing Machine Operation</>
      <option>Electrical Installation</option>
      </form>
    </body>
</html>
```

Your browser will display the following page with a drop-down menu:

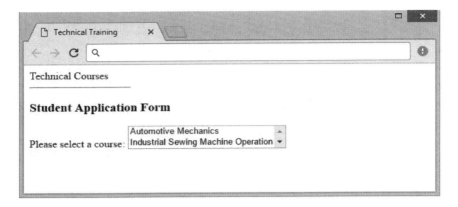

The container tag defines the individual items in dropdown menus. Here are the attributes for the <option></option> tag:

Attribute	Function	Values
value	Assigns a name to the dropdown menu item	text without spaces
selected	Indicates a default selected option	none

Email Feedback Form

Feedback forms facilitate communication with website visitors. The form allows them to submit comments and questions which will be sent to your email address.

Elements of a Feedback Form

A feedback from should have the following elements:

action="mailto:email address"	Sends the result to your email box
method="get"	Sends the forms as one request to the mail program
enctype="text/plain"	Converts the results to a readable file in your email box

Adding a Submit Button

A submit button submits the information input when clicked and is commonly found at the end of a form. It is created by typing submit as the value of the <input> type attribute. The value placed inside the value attribute indicates the button's label.

Example:

```
<!DOCTYPE html>
<html>
  <head>
    <title>Technical Training</title>
  </head>
    <body>
      <caption>Technical Courses</caption>
      <hr width="25%" align="left"/>
      <form action="action_page.php" method="post">
      <h3>Student Application Form</h3>
      <p>Please select a course:
      <select name="coursechoice" size="2"
      <option>Welding</option>
      <option>Automotive Mechanics</option>
      <option>Industrial Sewing Machine Operation</>
      <option>Electrical Installation</option>
      </select></font></p>
       Please click the Submit button to start sending your completed form.
       <p><input type="submit" value="Submit">
       <input type="reset" value="Reset"
      </form>
    </body>
</html>
```

Your browser will display the following form:

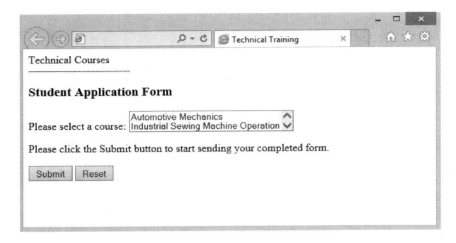

Adding a Reset Button

A Reset or Clear Button is usually found at the end of a form. It resets or clears all input data when clicked. You can create a Reset or Clear button by typing reset as the value of the input type attribute.

For example:

<input type="reset">

In addition, the value given to the value attribute indicates the button's label.

Password Field

HTML allows the creation of a password field into forms. The password characters are masked and are displayed as either black circles or asterisks.

For example, this code asks the user to type a name and a password:

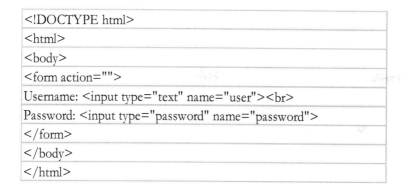

```
<!DOCTYPE html>
<html>
<body>
<form action="">
Username: <input type="text" name="user"><br>
Password: <input type="password" name="password">
</form>
</body>
</html>
```

Check out how the browser displays the password entered in asterisks:

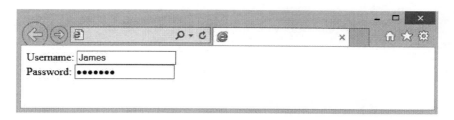

New Input Types in HTML5

HTML5 has introduced several new input types for HTML forms which provide better control over user input:

- number
- color
- date
- range
- month
- week
- time
- datetime-local
- datetime

91

- email
- search
- tel
- url

Input Type	Function
number	Specifies a numeric input field

The <input type="number"> is used to define an input that requires a number. It also allows web designers to set restrictions on the numbers that the input field can accept. Take note that it is not supported in IE9 and its earlier versions.

For example, the following code will display a numeric input field where the user can enter any value from 1 to 10:

```
<!DOCTYPE html>
<html>
<body>
  <form action="action_page.php">
  Quantity (from 1 to 10):
  <input type="number" name="quantity" min="1" max="10">
  <input type="submit">
  </form>
</body>
</html>
```

The following figure shows the output:

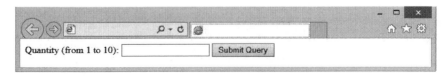

Input Restrictions

The following are the most common HTML input restrictions:

Input Type	Function
value	Defines the default value for input field
size	Specifies the width of an input field
max	Defines the maximum value allowed for an input field
min	Defines the minimum value allowed for an input field
maxlength	Defines the maximum length (number of characters) for an input field
readonly	Specifies a read only input field
step	Specifies the allowed intervals (in number) for an input field
disabled	Specifies a disabled input page
pattern	Specifies a regular expression against which the input value must be checked
required	Indicates that an input field must be filled out

Input Type	Function
color	Specifies an input field that requires a color

The <input type="color"> allows web designers to specify an input field that should contain a color. Internet Explorer 11 and Safari 9.1 and earlier versions of both web browsers do not support this input type. Some browsers, however, may allow a color picker to pop up when the user enters the input field.

Example:

```
<form>
  Choose your favorite color:
  <input type="color" name="favecolor">
</form>
```

Input Type	Function
date	Specifies an input field that requires a date

The <input type="date"> is used to define an input field that must contain a date. Take note that the date input type is not supported in IE 11 and its earlier versions as well as in Firefox. Other browsers may allow the date picker to pop up when the user enters the input field.

Example:

```
<!DOCTYPE html>
<html>
  <body>
  <form action>
   Membership Date:
   <input type="date" name="memday">
   <input type="submit">
   </form>
   </body>
   </html>
```

The figure below shows how the browser displays the above code. Notice that the date picker pops up when the user enters the input field:

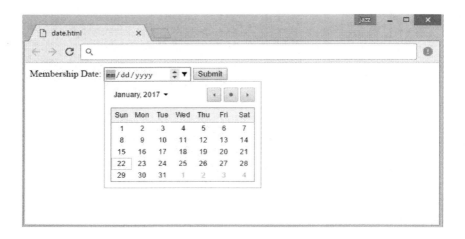

HTML allows you to specify restrictions to a date.

Example:

```
<form>
Enter a date before 2001-01-01:
  <input type="date" name="memday" max="2000-12-31"><br>
</form>
```

```
<form>
Enter a date after 2010-01-01:
  <input type="date" name="memday" min="2010-01-02"><br>
</form>
```

Input Type	Function
range	used when an input field requires a value within a range

The <input type="range"> is used when an input field needs a value within a range. Some browsers show the range input type as a slider control. IE 9 and its earlier versions do not support the range input type.

Example:

```
<!DOCTYPE html>
<html>
  <body>
    <form action="action_page.php" method="get">
    Bonus Points:
    <input type="range" name="bonuspoints" min="1"
    max="10">
    <input type="submit">
    </form>
  </body>
</html>
```

Here's what the browser may display:

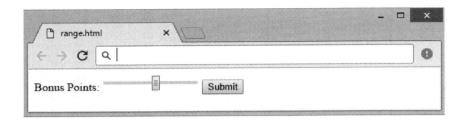

Input Type	Function
month	allows a user to choose the month and year

The <input type= "month"> is used for input fields that require the user to choose the month and year. Firefox and IE 11 and its earlier versions do not support the month input type. The date picker may pop up on other browsers that support this type.

Example:

```
<!DOCTYPE html>
<html>
  <body>
   <form>
   Anniversary (month, year):
    <input type="month" name="monthsary">
    <input type="submit">
   </form>

   </body>
</html>
```

This is how the browser will display the result:

96

Input Type	Function
week	allows a user to choose the week and year

The <input type= "week"> is used for input fields that ask the user to choose the week and year. Firefox and IE 11 and its earlier versions do not support this input type. The date picker may pop up on other browsers that support the week input type.

Example:

```
<!DOCTYPE html>
<html>
   <body>
   <form>
   Choose a week:
   <input type="week" name=" week_year">
   <input type="submit">
   </form>
   </body>
</html>
```

Input Type	Function
time	asks the user to select a time

The <input type= "time"> is used for input fields that ask the user to choose the time. Firefox and IE 12 and its earlier versions do not support the time input type. The time picker may pop up on other browsers that support this type.

Example:

```
<!DOCTYPE html>
<html>
   <body>
   <form>
```

```
  Choose a time:
  <input type="time" name="usr_time">
  <input type="submit">
  </form>

  </body>
</html>
```

Input Type	Function
datetime-local	creates an input field for selecting date and time

The <input type= "datetime-local"> is used to specify an input field that asks the user to select the date and the time. Firefox and IE 12 and its earlier versions do not support the datetime input type. A date picker may pop up on other browsers that support this input type.

Example:

```
<!DOCTYPE html>
<html>
  <body>
  <form>
    Birthday (date, time):
    <input type="datetime-local" name="bdatetime">
    <input type="submit" value="Submit">
  </form>
  </body>
</html>
```

Input Type	Function
email	specifies an input field that requires an e-mail address

The <input type= "email"> is used to specify an input field that ask the user to enter an email address. The Internet Explorer 9 and its earlier versions do not support this input type.

Example:

```
<!DOCTYPE html>
<html>
  <body>
  <form>
  Email address:
  <input type="email" name="email">
  <input type="submit">
  </form>
  </body>
</html>
```

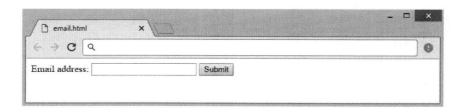

Input Type	Function
search	specifies a search field

The <input type="search"> is used to specify a search field.

Example:

```
<!DOCTYPE html>
<html>
  <body>
  <form>
   Search Google:
   <input type="search" name="searchgoogle">
   <input type="send">
   </form>
   </body>
</html>
```

Input Type	Function
tel	used to specify an input field that requires a telephone number

The <input type="tel"> is used to define a field that requires a telephone number. Currently, only Safari 8 and its more recent versions support this input type.

Example:

```
<!DOCTYPE html>
<html>
<body>
<form>
 Telephone:
 <input type="tel" name="telno">
 <input type="submit">
</form>
</body>
</html>
```

Input Type	Function
url	specifies an input field that requires a URL address

The <input type="url"> is used to define a field that requires a URL address. Internet Explorer 9 and its earlier versions do not support the url input type. Other browsers may automatically validate the field when submitted.

Example:

```
<!DOCTYPE html>
<html>
  <body>
  <form>
   Enter your homepage:
   <input type="url" name="urhomepage">
   <input type="submit">
   </form>
   </body>
</html>
```

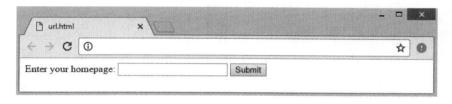

HTML Entities

Some characters are reserved and should not be used in your codes to avoid errors or mishandling. For instance, if you use the greater than (>) or less than (<) signs in your text, the browser will most likely confuse them with tags.

Character entities are used to show HTML reserved characters.

Here's an example:

&entity_name;
OR

&#entity_number;

101

CHAPTER 12: HTML LAYOUT ELEMENTS

Website content is frequently displayed in multiple columns format. HTML5 features new semantic elements that you can use to define the different sections of a web page.

<header>	Defines a header for a section or document
<section>	Defines a section in a document
<article>	Defines an independent article
<nav>	Defines a container for navigation links
<aside>	Defines content aside from the content (like a sidebar)
<details>	Defines additional details
<summary>	Defines a heading for the <details> element
<footer>	Defines a footer for a document or a section

HTML Layout Techniques

There are four ways to create layouts with multiple columns:.

- HTML tables
- CSS framework
- CSS flexbox
- CSS float property

HTML Tables

The HTML <table> element was not intended to be layout tool. Its purpose is simply to display data in tabular format. To avoid the hassles of redesigning your website, you should avoid using tables to style your web page.

CHAPTER 13: HTML MULTIMEDIA

Multimedia includes sound, videos, music, images, movies, and animations. These elements are stored in media files in different formats and extensions. You can easily identify the file format by looking at the extension.

Video Files

There are two ways to add videos to your website: the <embed> tag and the <video> tag.

The <embed> tag

You can use the following video types inside the <embed> tag:

.wmv	Windows Media Video format by Microsoft
.swf	Macromedia Flash file type
.mpeg	Moving Pictures Expert Group video file type
.mov	Quick Time Movie format by Apple

Attributes for the <embed> tag:

Attribute	Function	Values
align	Specifies the alignment of the object file	left, center, right
autostart	Specifies if the media should play automatically	True, False
loop	Indicates if the sound should play continuously	true, number, false

playcount	Indicates the number of time a sound should be played	number
hidden	Indicates if a multimedia object should be displayed or not	true(yes), false(no)
width	Specifies the object's width in pixels	number
height	Specifies the object's height in pixels	number
name	A name for the object	text without spaces
src	Indicates the URL of the object to be embedded.	
volume	Controls volume of the sound	0 to 100

The <embed> tag can be used to play a Youtube video directly on your web page. Here are the steps:

1. Open the Youtube video that you want to use on your page.
2. Click on share at the bottom of the video to see the embed link.
3. The page will display the HTML code.
4. Copy and paste the code on your HTML document.

Example:

```
<!DOCTYPE html>
<html>
<head>
  <title>Mr. Bean</title>
</head>
<body>
<embed
<iframe                    width="560"                    height="315"
src="https://www.youtube.com/embed/FV80V8S3iU4"    frameborder="0"
allowfullscreen></iframe>
  </embed>
</body>
</html>
```

The \<video> Tag

The HTML5 \<video> tag is used to insert a video to a web page. The new \<video> tag is widely supported by major browsers such as Chrome, Internet Explorer, Firefox, Safari, and Opera. It is not, however, supported by IE 8 and earlier versions.

Currently, HTML5 supports the following video types:

Format	Extension
MP4 or MPEG-4	.mp4
WebM	.webm
Ogg	.ogg

The following are the attributes of the \<video> tag:

Attribute	Function	Values
autoplay	Specifies that the video will start playing automatically	autoplay
controls	Specifies whether video controls should be displayed	controls
height	Specifies the video player's height	pixels

loop	Specifies that the video will play continuously	loop
muted	Specifies that the video audio output should be muted	muted
poster	Specifies an image to be displayed while waiting for the video to play	URL
preload	Specifies if the video should be loaded as the page loads and how	auto, metadata, none
src	Specifies the URL of the video file	URL
width	Sets the video player's width in pixels	pixels

When using the <video> tag on your page, you need to specify the height and width attributes for the video to reserve the space it needs when the webpage is loaded.

Take note that when you use a browser that do not support the video tag, it will display the text between the start and end video tags. You must insert a text between the <video></video> tags to inform your viewers why it does not play as expected.

For example, if you want to play a video stored in the local drive, you will have to specify the drive and the filename:

```
<!DOCTYPE html>
<html>
<body>
<video width="320" height="240" controls>
  <source src=c/dinosaur.mp4 type="video/mp4">
  Your browser does not support the video tag.
</video>
</body>
</html>
```

If your browser supports the video tag, you will likely see a video like this one:

106

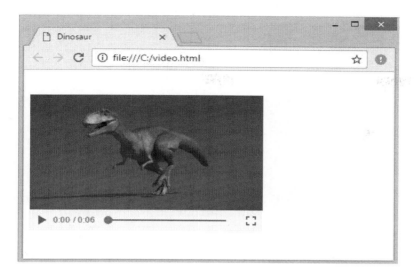

Adding Audio

HTML5 introduced the <audio> tag and like the <video> tag, it easily gained wide acceptance among modern browsers.

HTML5 supports these audio types:

Format	Extension
MP3	.mp3
WAV	.wav
Ogg	.ogg

Example:

```
<!DOCTYPE html>
<html>
  <header>
    <title> </title>
  <header>
  <body>
    <audio controls="controls">
      <source src=c:/music.mp3 type="audio/mpeg" />
    Your browser does not support this audio type.
```

```
      </audio>
  </body>
  <html>
```

Tag	Function
<audio>	Defines sound content
<source>	Defines resources for multimedia elements such audio and video

Linking a Webpage to Audio or Video Files

If you want Youtube videos to play when your visitor clicks a video, you can link the video files to your webpage.

Here is an example:

```
<!DOCTYPE!>
<html>
  <head>
    <title>Mr. Bean</title>
  </head>
  <body>
    <hl>Mr. Bean</hl>
<p>
<a
href="https://www.youtube.com/watch?v=sfx6AdOZc7w&list=CLOP3DshNr
h-Y">Mr. Bean – The Leaky Goldfish</a>
</p>
  </body>
</html>
```

Your web page will have a clickable link like this one:

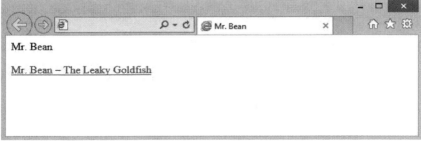

CHAPTER 14: CSS3

CSS means Cascading Style Sheets. CSS was created to simplify the process of designing and presenting web pages. It is an easy-to-learn design language that offers powerful control over the presentation of HTML documents. It is usually combined with HTML or XHTML. CSS3 is the latest version of CSS.

Why You Should Use CSS

CSS lets you save time. You can write one style sheet and define a style for each element and apply it to several HTML pages.

Faster loading time. If you're using CSS, you need not create HTML tag attributes all the time. You just have to write a CSS style for a tag and apply it to each occurrence of that tag. This means less code which translates to faster loading time.

Fast and easy maintenance. When you need to implement a global change, you'll just have to change the style and that will automatically update all elements in your web pages.

Superior styling options. Compared to HTML, CSS offers a wider array of style options. This will empower you to provide a much better look to your HTML pages than what your HTML attributes can provide.

Compatibility across multiple devices. Style sheets let you optimize your content for several types of devices. With just one HTML document, you can present different versions of your website for handheld devices such as cellphones or PDAs.

Compliance with global web standards. Many HTML attributes have been removed and for your HTML pages to be compatible with modern and future browsers, you should start using CSS.

Offline browsing. By using an offline cache, CSS stores web applications locally and allows you to view offline web pages. The cache likewise facilitates faster loading time and better performance for the website.

Platform Independence. The CSS script provides platform independence and supports the latest browsers.

CSS3 is the latest version of Cascading Style Sheets. It introduced many new properties that are currently being implemented in most browsers. The following are CSS3's most important modules:

- Selectors
- Text effects
- Backgrounds and borders
- Box model
- 2D/3D transformations
- Animations
- Multiple column layout
- User interface
- Image values and replaced content

CSS Syntax and Selectors

A CSS style rule consists of two major parts:

1. selector

A selector is the HTML tag or element that will be styled. It could be any tag like <table>, <p>, or <h1>. You can specify several selectors over which the style may be applied.

2. declaration block

A declaration block consists of a property:value pair and each pair are separated by a colon. A CSS property points to an HTML attribute and can include color, border, etc. A value is assigned to each property declared. A declaration block is enclosed by curly braces and may contain one or more declarations which are separated by semicolons.

Here's an example of a rule set:

h1 {color:red; font-size:10px}

CSS Selectors

Selectors are used to specify HTML elements based on their id, name, attribute, class, etc. There are different ways to define CSS selectors and you can choose whichever you need or whatever feels more convenient.

The Element Selector

The element selector uses the element's name as the basis for implementing a style.

For example:
```
p {
    text-align: left;
    color: blue;
}
```

The above style rule will result in all <p> elements to be left-aligned with a blue text color.

ID Selector

ID selectors name an element's id attribute as the basis for implementing a style set. An element with that ID will be formatted according to its style rule. To use the ID selector, you will write a hash (#) character before the element's ID.

For example, the following style rule will apply to an element with the id of "parax":

```
#parax {
    text-align: left;
    color: blue;
}
```

Class Selector

Class selectors are used to format elements with a particular class attribute. The style rule you define will apply to all elements that match the specified class. To use the class selector, you will write a period (.) before the class name.

For example, in the following code, all HTML elements with class="black" will be blue and left-aligned:

```
.black {
    text-align: left;
    color: blue;
}
```

The Descendant Selectors

The descendant selector is used to select a specific element within an element. For example, the style rule below will only apply to <em> element that lies inside the <ol> tag:

```
ol em {
    color: red;
}
```

The Universal Selector

The universal selector is used to select the name of all element types. In the following example, all elements will be presented in blue:

```
* {
  color:blue;
}
```

The Child Selectors

The child selector selects an element for formatting only if they are a direct child of an element. For example:

```
body > p {
  color: blue;
}
```

The style rule will cause all paragraphs directly under the body element to be presented in blue. The style rule will not affect paragraphs placed inside other elements such as <td> or <div>.

The Attribute Selectors

The attribute selector selects elements with specific attributes for formatting.

For example:

```
input[type = "text"]{
  color: black;
}
```

The above style will only apply to the element with the specified attribute input type="text".

113

Grouping Selectors

CSS lets you to apply a single style to multiple selectors. This feature will save you lines of codes and time. You just need to separate the selectors with a comma.

For example:

h1, h2, h3 {

    letter-spacing: .6em;
    font-weight: normal;
    color: black;
    text-transform: lowercase;
    margin-bottom: 1.5em;
}

The defined style rule will apply to the elements h1, h2, and h3.

Inserting a Style Sheet

There are three ways to insert a style sheet: external style sheet, internal style sheet, and inline style.

External Style Sheets

An external style sheet allows you to change the look of multiple pages and the layout of your entire website by simply changing a single file. Any modification made to the external style sheet instantly updates all web pages.

The external style sheet is implemented by making a reference to the file inside the link element placed within the <head> section of the HTML page.

For example:

```
<!DOCTYPE html>
<html>
<head>
<link rel="stylesheet" type="text/css" href="myownstyle.css">
</head>
<body>
<p>This is a space for a paragraph.</p>
</body>
</html>
```

Just like an HTML page, you can write an external style sheet using any text editor. The file must be saved with a .css extension and should not contain HTML tags.

Here is how the myownstle.css might look:

```
body {
    background-color: lightblue;
}

h1 {
    color: navy;
    margin-left: 35px;
}
```

Creating an External CSS File

External style sheets, also called linked styles, are created outside the HTML file and linked. The <link> element which is placed inside the <head></head> section of the HTML document tells the browser to search for the specified style sheet.

A CSS style sheet is a file that contains nothing but styles. Just like HTML files, you can create style sheet with any text editor. You have to save the file with the .css file extension and select the All Files option.

The following steps will demonstrate how you can create and test a basic style sheet. You will save your file and view your output in the browser:

- Create a new document in Notepad.
- Type the style that you want to implement.
- On the Menu Bar, click on File and choose Save As.
- Type your file name and use the file extension .css.
- Change the file type to All Files.
- Choose Save.

To demonstrate, create a new folder inside your website or HTML files folder and name it 'style'. Create the following file and save it as mystyle.css inside the HTML/style folder:

```
p{
color:blue;
}
```

Linking CSS File to an HTML File

After creating a CSS file, open your HTML file.

Type the following inside the head section of your HTML file:

```
<link rel="stylesheet" type="text/css" href="myownstyle.css">
```

Save your modified HTML file.

To demonstrate, the following code shows how you can link the myownstyle.css file to an HTML document:

```
<head>
    <title>Dog Breeds</title>
    <link rel="stylesheet" type="text/css" href="myownstyle.css">
</head>
<body>
```

```
<font size="5">
<h3 align="center">Top Dog Breeds</h3>

<p align="justify"> A Siberian Husky is a working dog with various coat
markings and colors. The Pug is a breed with a wrinkly face, short square muzzle,
and curly tail. The German Shepherd Dog is an intelligent working dog with a
protective attitude.</p>
    </font>
<body>
```

Below is the modified web page showing the paragraph text in blue font:

Internal Style Sheets

An internal style sheet is commonly used when you want to present a page in a different style. It is defined inside the <style> element placed within the <head> and </head> tags of the HTML page.

For example, the following code uses an internal style sheet to create a pink background for the entire page and a heading in green font:

```
<head>
  <title>Dog Breeds</title>
  <style>
    body {
    background-color: pink;
    }
    h3 {
```

```
       color: green;
       margin-left:40px;
       }
   </style>
</head>
<body>
   <font size="5">
   <h3 align="center">Top Dog Breeds</h3>
   <p align="justify"> A Siberian Husky is a working dog with
various coat markings and colors. The Pug is a breed with a wrinkly
face, short square muzzle, and curly tail. The German Shepherd
Dog is an intelligent working dog with a   protective attitude.</p>
   </font>
   <body>
</html>
```

Here's the result:

Inline Style Sheets

An inline style is commonly used to apply a unique style or isolated changes to a single element such as a headline, paragraph, or other element. The use of inline style will override both external and internal style sheets. To use it, you have to add the style attribute to the specific element.

Example:

<!DOCTYPE html>

118

```
<html>
<body>
<h1 style="color:yellow;margin-left:25px;">This space is reserved for a heading.
</h1>
<p>This is a space for a paragraph.</p>
</body>
</html>
```

When specifying style to an element, you can use as many attributes as you like as long as you separate them with a semi-colon and provide the proper syntax for the values.

To illustrate, the following code will style the heading with red font and left margin of 25px and paragraph text using Arial font in green text color:

```
<head>
    <title>Dog Breeds</title>
</head>
<body>
    <font size="5">
    <h3 align="center" style="color:red; margin-left:25px;">Top
Dog Breeds</h3>
    <p align="justify" style=> A Siberian Husky is a working dog
with various coat markings and colors. The Pug is a breed with a
wrinkly face, short square muzzle, and curly tail. The German
Shepherd Dog is an intelligent working dog with a    protective
attitude.</p>
    </font>
<body>
```

This is how the browser will display the webpage:

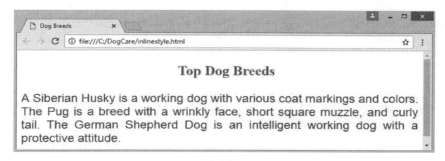

119

Take note that when you use the inline style to design your document, the style sheet loses most of its advantages. Hence, it is not considered as the best way to take advantage of the formatting features of CSS3.

Cascading Order

When you define more than one style for an HTML element, all styles will cascade into new virtual style sheets using the following order of priority:

- Inline style (inside an HTML element)
- External and internal style sheets (head section)
- Browser default

Thus, when you place an inline style inside an HTML element, it will be given the highest priority in implementation and will override other designs.

CHAPTER 15: STYLING TEXT

CSS offers much more style and effects than HTML. With its text styling properties, you can set the color, alignment, decoration, case, height, indent, letter and word spacing, and direction.

Text Properties

Property	Function	Values
color	Indicates the color of the text	color name, code, hexadecimal value, RGB
text-indent	Sets the indentation of the first line of a paragraph or text block	length, number of pixels (px), percentage (%)
text-shadow	Specifies the shadow effect applied to text	color, length, inherit, none
text-align	Sets the horizontal alignment of the text	justify, right, center, left
vertical-align	Specifies the vertical alignment	baseline, super, sub, top, bottom, middle
text-decoration	Specifies the decoration applied to the text	line-through, overline, underline, blink, super, sub, none
text-transform	Sets the text capitalization	capitalize, uppercase, lowercase, none
line-height	Specifies the line height	normal, number of pixels (px), percentage (%)
letter-spacing	Adjusts the spaces between characters	length, number of pixels (px),

		normal
word-spacing	Adjusts the space between words	length, number of pixels (px), normal
white-space	Indicates how the white space is handled	normal, nowrap, pre
direction	Specifies the text/writing direction	rtl (right to left), ltr (left to right), inherit
text-overflow	Sets how overflowed content should be indicated to the user	
unicode-bidi	Sets or returns whether the text should be overridden to support the other languages on a single document	

CSS Fonts

The font properties specify the font family, size, boldness, and style of text. Having two or more font types on your website code is a good practice as some browsers may not support a particular font family. In such case, the browser will simply select the next font in line.

Font Families

CSS recognizes two font families:

generic family   collection of font families with similar appearance
font family   refers to a particular font family such as 'Arial' or 'Georgia'.

The generic family are categorized into serif, sans-serif, and monospace.

Serif   The serif group of fonts are distinguished by small lines at the end of some characters. It includes font families like Georgia and Times New Roman.

Sans-serif   The sans-serif group of fonts are those that have no lines at the end of the characters. It includes Arial and Verdana.

Monospace   The monospace group of fonts have the same width for all characters. It includes Lucida Console and Courier New.

Font Properties

Property	Function	Values
font	Sets all font properties in a single declaration	values available to other font properties
font-style	Specifies text font style	Italics, Normal, Oblique
font-family	Specifies the type face for text	Ex: Serif, Georgia, Times New Roman
font-size	Sets the font size	normal, xx-small, x-small, small, medium, large, x-large, xx-large; number used with % (percent), pt (points), or px (pixels)
font-variant	Specifies if a text should be displayed in small-caps font	normal, small-caps, initial, inherit
font-weight	Specifies the thinness or thickness of characters in text	normal, bold, bolder, lighter, a number from 100 to 900

Creating an Italic Text

The font-style property is used to display the text in italic, oblique, or normal.

For example, your CSS code might look like this:

```
p {
font-style:italic;
 }
h4 {
font-style:oblique;
 }
```

You can save the above css code as fontstyle.css and link it to an HTML document with the following code:

```
<head>
  <title>Dog Breeds</title>
  <link rel="stylesheet" href="style/fontstyle.css" type="text/css"/>
</head>
<body>
  <h4 align="center"> Popular Dog Breeds </h4>
  <p> The Shih Tzu is a strong and sturdy toy dog with a sweet-natured temperament. </p>
  <p> The Bulldog is a sturdy medium-sized dog with a wrinkled mug and a distinctive underbite.</p>
   <p> The Yorkshire Terrier is a tiny dog with an inquisitive temperament and stunning coat.</p>
</body>
```

Your browser will display the following:

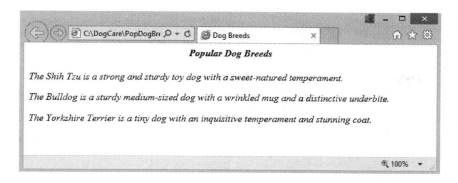

Creating a Bold Text

You can display a text in bold by using the font-weight property. This property allows you to set the text to bold, bolder, lighter, or normal. You may also adjust the boldness level by specifying a number from 100 to 900.

For example, you can create a new css file, myfontstyle2.css, with the following style:

```
p {
font-weight:bold;
}
h4
font-weight:800;
}
```

You can link this new file to your html document with the following code:

```
<head>
    <title>Dog Breeds</title>
        <link rel="stylesheet" href="style/fontstyle.css" type="text/css"/>
        <link rel="stylesheet" href="style/fontstyle2.css" type="text/css"/>
</head>
<body>
    <h4 align="center"> Popular Dog Breeds </h4>
    <p> The Shih Tzu is a strong and sturdy toy dog with a sweet-natured temperament. </p>
```

```
    <p> The Bulldog is a sturdy medium-sized dog with a wrinkled mug and a
distinctive underbite.</p>
    <p> The Yorkshire Terrier is a tiny dog with an inquisitive temperament and
stunning coat.</p>
</body>
```

This is what your browser will display:

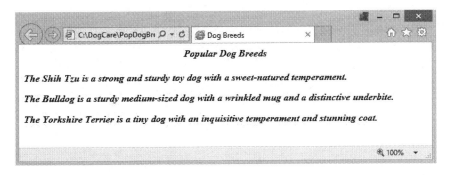

Indenting Text

The text-indent property is used to indent the first line of text block or paragraph. You can specify the indentation in percentage of the text block width in px, cm, mm, pt, in, pc, em, or ex.

To illustrate, create a new css file and save it as indentstyle.css:

```
p {
text-indent: 40px
}
```

Link the indentstyle.css to the HTML document:

```
<head>
   <title>Dog Breeds</title>
   <link rel="stylesheet" href="style/fontstyle.css" type="text/css"/>
   <link rel="stylesheet" href="style/indentstyle.css" type="text/css"/>
</head>
<body>
   <h4 align="center"> Popular Dog Breeds </h4>
```

```
<p> The Shih Tzu is a strong and sturdy toy dog with a sweet-natured
temperament. </p>
<p> The Bulldog is a sturdy medium-sized dog with a wrinkled mug and a
distinctive underbite.</p>
<p> The Yorkshire Terrier is a tiny dog with an inquisitive temperament and
stunning coat.</p>
    </body>
</html>
```

Here's what your browser will display:

Changing the Font

To change the font, you will use the CSS font-family property. Since not all fonts are supported, you must specify a second choice. You can also opt to use common fonts such as Arial, Times New Roman, or Verdana.

For example, create a new css file and save it as fontstyle3.css:

```
p {
font-familly:verdana, georgia;
}
h4 {
font-family:georgia, Times New Roman;
}
```

Link the fontstyle3.css file with the HTML document:

127

```
<head>
  <title>Dog Breeds</title>
  <link rel="stylesheet" href="style/fontstyle2.css" type="text/css"/>
  <link rel="stylesheet" href="style/fontstyle3.css" type="text/css"/>
</head>
<body>
  <h4 align="center"> Popular Dog Breeds </h4>
  <p> The Shih Tzu is a strong and sturdy toy dog with a sweet-natured
temperament. </p>
    <p> The Bulldog is a sturdy medium-sized dog with a wrinkled mug and a
distinctive underbite.</p>
    <p> The Yorkshire Terrier is a tiny dog with an inquisitive temperament and
stunning coat.</p>
</body>
```

This is how the browser will display your webpage:

Changing the Font Size

The font-size property is used to change the font size. You can use units such as pt, px, mm, cm, pc, in, ex, or em. You may also opt to use descriptions such as xx-small, x-small, small, medium, large, x-large, or xx-large.

For example, create a new css file and save it as fontstyle4:

```
p {
font-size:xx-large;
}
```

128

The css file changes the font size from the default to xx-large. Now, link the fontstyle4.css to the HTML document with this code:

```
<head>
    <title>Dog Breeds</title>

    <link rel="stylesheet" href="style/fontstyle4.css" type="text/css"/>
    <link rel="stylesheet" href="style/fontstyle3.css" type="text/css"/>
</head>
<body>
    <h4 align="center"> Popular Dog Breeds </h4>
    <p> The Shih Tzu is a strong and sturdy toy dog with a sweet-natured
temperament. </p>
    <p> The Bulldog is a sturdy medium-sized dog with a wrinkled mug and a
distinctive underbite.</p>
    <p> The Yorkshire Terrier is a tiny dog with an inquisitive temperament
and stunning coat.</p>
</body>
```

This is how the browser will display the webpage:

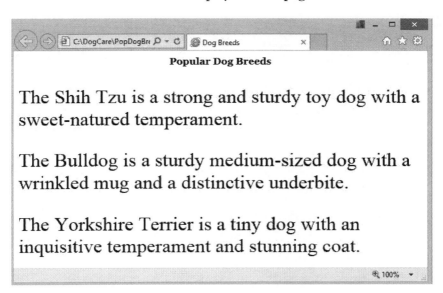

Changing the Text Case

The text transform property is used to set the text case. You can use options such as capitalize, uppercase, lowercase, or none.

For example, create a new css file and save it as fontstyle5:

```
h4 {
text-transform:uppercase;
}
```

Link the fontstyle5.css with the HTML document:

```
<head>
  <title>Dog Breeds</title>
      <link rel="stylesheet" href="style/fontstyle3.css" type="text/css"/>
      <link rel="stylesheet" href="style/fontstyle5.css" type="text/css"/>
</head>
<body>
    <h4 align="center"> Popular Dog Breeds </h4>
    <p> The Shih Tzu is a strong and sturdy toy dog with a sweet-natured temperament. </p>
    <p> The Bulldog is a sturdy medium-sized dog with a wrinkled mug and a distinctive underbite.</p>
    <p> The Yorkshire Terrier is a tiny dog with an inquisitive temperament and stunning coat.</p>
</body>
```

Here's how the webpage will look:

Transforming Text

The text transformation property is used to specify uppercase and lowercase letters.

For example:

```
p.capitalize {text-transform:capitalize}
p.uppercase {text-transform:lowercase}
p.lowercase text-transform:uppercase}
```

Changing Text Alignment

The text-align property is used to change the alignment of the text. You can set the text alignment to left, right, center, and justified.

Example:

Create a new css file and save it as style3.css:

```
h2 {
text-align:center;
}
p{
text-align:right;
}
```

Link the style3.css to your HTML document:

```
<head>
    <title>Dog Breeds</title>
    <link rel="stylesheet" href="style/fontstyle3.css" type="text/css"/>
    <link rel="stylesheet" href="style/style3.css" type="text/css"/>
</head>
<body>
    <h3 align="center"> Popular Dog Breeds </h3>
    <p> The Shih Tzu is a strong and sturdy toy dog with a sweet-natured temperament. </p>
    <p> The Bulldog is a sturdy medium-sized dog with a wrinkled mug and a distinctive underbite.</p>
```

131

```
<p> The Yorkshire Terrier is a tiny dog with an inquisitive temperament
and stunning coat.</p>
</body>
```

You should see this figure on your browser:

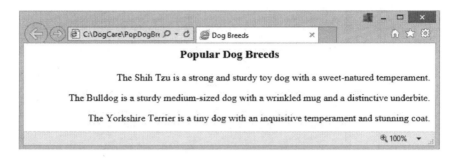

Changing Line Spacing

The line-height property is used to set line spacing.

For example, create a new css file and save it as style4:

```
p {
line-height:3;
}
```

Link style4.css with the HTML document:

```
<head>
   <title>Dog Breeds</title>
       <link rel="stylesheet" href="style/fontstyle3.css" type="text/css"/>
       <link rel="stylesheet" href="style/style4.css" type="text/css"/>
</head>
<body>
     <h3 align="center"> Popular Dog Breeds </h3>
     <p text-align="justify"> The Shih Tzu is a strong and sturdy toy dog with a
sweet-natured temperament. </p>
     <p text-align="justify"> The Bulldog is a sturdy medium-sized dog with a
wrinkled mug and a distinctive underbite.</p>
```

```
    <p text-align="justify"> The Yorkshire Terrier is a tiny dog with an
inquisitive temperament and stunning coat.</p>
    </body>
</html>
```

This is how the webpage should appear on the browser:

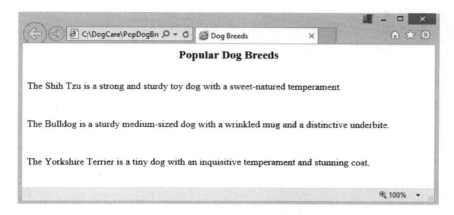

Adding Text Decoration

The text-decoration property is used to add or remove decorations from text.

The values 'line-through', 'overline', 'underline', and 'blink' are used to add decorations to text:

```
h1 {
    text-decoration: line-through;
}

h2 {
    text-decoration: overline;
}

h4 {
    text-decoration: underline;
}
h6 {
```

text-decoration:blink;

The value 'none' is commonly used to remove underlines from link text:

a {text-decoration: none;}

Example:

```
<head>
    <style>
    h2 {
    text-decoration: overline;
    }

    h3 {
    text-decoration: line-through;
    }

    h4 {
    text-decoration: underline;
    }
    </style>
</head>
<body>
  <h2>Dog Breeds</h2>
  <h3>Top Dog Breeds</h3>
  <h4>Popular Dog Breeds</h4>
</body>
```

134

Here's an example of a link text that has no underline:

```
<head>
 <style>
   a {
      text-decoration: none;
      }
 </style>
</head>
<body>

 <p>This link has no underline: <a href="https://en.wikipedia.org/wiki/Dog">wikipedia.org/wiki/Dog </a></p>

</body>
```

Changing the Text Color

You will make use of the color property to change the color of the text. The World Wide Web Consortium had listed sixteen valid color names for HTML and CSS. You may also use the other 150 color names that are supported by the major browsers. If you want to use other colors, you have to use the hex value.

For example, create a new css file and save it as style6:

```
h3 {
color:blue;
}
p {
color:green;
}
```

Link style6.css to your document:

```
<head>
```

```
    <title>Dog Breeds</title>
    <link rel="stylesheet" href="style/fontstyle3.css" type="text/css"/>
    <link rel="stylesheet" href="style/style6.css" type="text/css"/>
</head>
<body>
    <h3 align="center"> Popular Dog Breeds </h3>
    <p text-align="justify"> The Shih Tzu is a strong and sturdy toy dog with a
sweet-natured temperament. </p>
    <p text-align="justify"> The Bulldog is a sturdy medium-sized dog with a
wrinkled mug and a distinctive underbite.</p>
    <p text-align="justify"> The Yorkshire Terrier is a tiny dog with an
inquisitive temperament and stunning coat.</p>
</body>
```

This is how Google Chrome will display the webpage:

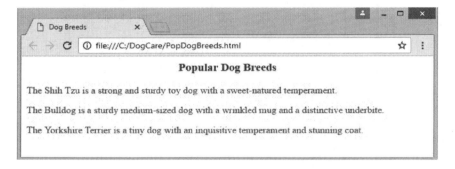

Adding a Background Color to a Text

The CSS background property is used to add a color behind a text without changing the webpage's background.

For example, create a new css file and name is style7.css:

```
h3{
    background:aqua;
    }
p{color:blue;
    }
```

Link style7.css to the HTML file:

136

```
<head>
    <title>Dog Breeds</title>

    <link rel="stylesheet" href="style/fontstyle3.css" type="text/css"/>
    <link rel="stylesheet" href="style/style7.css" type="text/css"/>
</head>
<body>
    <h3 align="center"> Popular Dog Breeds </h3>
    <p text-align="justify"> The Shih Tzu is a strong and sturdy toy dog with a
sweet-natured temperament. </p>
    <p text-align="justify"> The Bulldog is a sturdy medium-sized dog with a
wrinkled mug and a distinctive underbite.</p>
    <p text-align="justify"> The Yorkshire Terrier is a tiny dog with an
inquisitive temperament and stunning coat.</p>
</body>
```

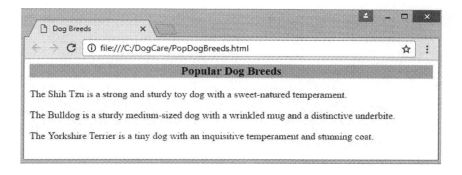

CSS3 Text

CSS3 introduced the features text-overflow, word-wrap, and word-break.

Text Overflow

The text-overflow property is used to define how you want to alert users about overflowed content.

Overflowed content can be clipped or rendered as ellipsis.

The following code illustrates how the text-overflow property is used:

```
<style>
p.text1 {

    width: 180px;
    border: 2px solid red;
    white-space: nowrap;
    overflow: hidden;
    text-overflow: clip;
}

p.text2 {
    width: 180px;
    border: 2px solid red;
    white-space: nowrap;
    overflow: hidden;
    text-overflow: ellipsis;
}
</style>
</head>
<body>

<p>Long text that does not fit inside the box.</p>

<p>text-overflow:clip:</p>
<p class="text1">The battery functions as the power source of the ignition system and a voltage stabilizer.</p>

<p>text-overflow: ellipsis:</p>
<p class="text2">The battery functions as the power source of the ignition system and a voltage stabilizer.</p>
```

Here's how the text will appear:

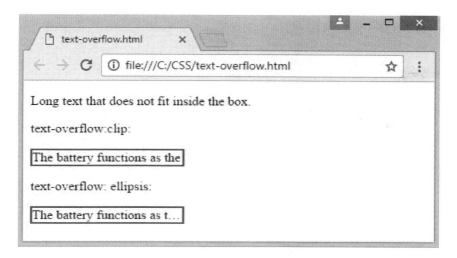

The following code illustrates how overflowed content can be displayed while hovering over it:

```
<head>
<style>
div.text1 {
    white-space: nowrap;
    width: 180px;
    overflow: hidden;
    border: 2px solid orange;
}

div.text1:hover {
    text-overflow: inherit;
    overflow: visible;
}
</style>
</head>
<body>

<p>Hover over the divs to view the whole text.</p>
<div class="text1" style="text-overflow:clip;">A battery fuctions as the power
source of the ignition system and a voltage stabilizer.</div>
<div class="text1" style="text-overflow:ellipsis;">A battery function as the
power source of the ignition system and a voltage stabilizer.</div>
<br>

</body>
```

Here's the result:

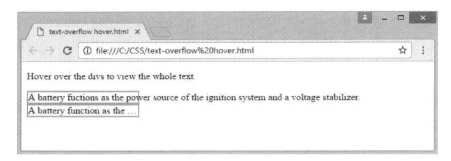

Word Wrapping

The word-wrap property lets you set long words to be broken and wrapped to the next line(s). A long word that can't fit inside an area can be set to expand outside or can be forced to wrap by splitting it in the middle.

Here's an example:

```
<!DOCTYPE html>
<html>
  <head>
    <style>
      p.text1 {
      width: 12em;
      border: 2px solid green;
      word-wrap: break-word;
      }
    </style>
  </head>
  <body>

    <p     class="text1">    This     block     contains     a
veryveryveryveryveryveryconfidentialword that will break amd wrap to the next
line.</p>
  </body>
</html>
```

Here's the result:

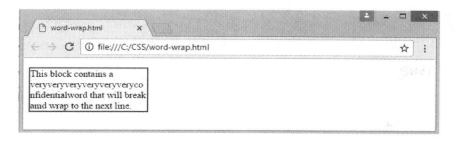

Word Breaking

The word-break property is used to specify line breaking rules.

Here's a code that will illustrate how to set this property to break a text at a hyphen or at any other character:

```
<!DOCTYPE html>
<html>
  <head>
    <style>
      p.text1 {
      width: 130px;
      border: 2px solid blue;
      word-break: keep-all;
      }

      p.text2 {
      width: 130px;
      border: 2px solid blue;
      word-break: break-all;
      }
    </style>
  </head>
  <body>

    <p class="text1">How do you break jacks-in-the-box-with-extended-hypens text?</p>

    <p class="text2">How do you break jacks-in-the-box-with-extended-hypens text?</p>

  </body>
</html>
```

Here's the result:

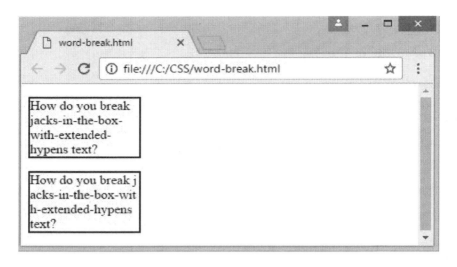

CHAPTER 16: FORMATTING LAYOUT

The Box Model

In HTML, you can consider any element as a box. In CSS, 'box model' refers to a website's style and layout. A box model in CSS consists of content, padding, border, and margin. They wrap around each HTML element.

The box model lets designers define space between each element and to add borders around them.

Below is an illustration of the box model:

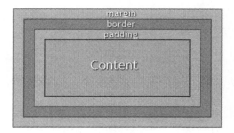

The content is the part of the box where the text and images appear. The padding is transparent and it clears the area around the content. The border wraps around the content and the padding. The margin is transparent and clears the area around the border.

When setting the height and width of an element's properties, you simply set the content area's height and width. To get the full size, you also have to consider the borders, padding, and margins.

For instance, if you want to style your element to have a total width of 300px, you have to specify the measurements that will add up to 300px as in the following example:

width:260px;
padding:5px;
border:10px solid blue;
margin:5px

This is how it all adds up for the width element:

260px (content area width)
10px (5px right padding + 5px left padding)
20px (10px right border + 10px left border)
10px (5px right margin +5px left margin)
= 300px total

Below are the formula for calculating the width and height of an element:

Total element width:

width + left and right padding + left and right border + left and right margin

Total element width = width + left padding + right padding + left border + right border + left margin and right margin

Total element height:

height + top and bottom padding + top and bottom border + top and bottom margin

The following code illustrates how you can set the height and width of a <div> element:

<!DOCTYPE html>

```
<html>
<head>
<style>
div {
    width: 250px;
    padding: 15px;
    border: 10px solid gray;
    margin: 0px;
}
</style>
</head>
<body>

<h2>Setting the total width:</h2>

<img src="style/poodle.jpg" width="300" height="250" alt="poodle">
<div>The above image is 300px wide and the total width of this element is
likewise 300px.</div>

</body>
</html>
```

The image below shows the outcome of the width setting code:

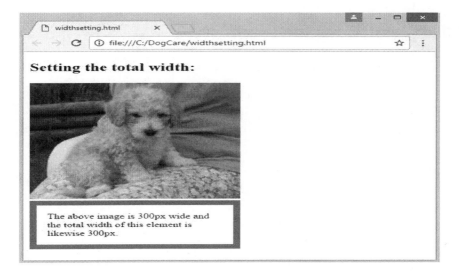

CSS Outline

An outline refers to the lines drawn around the elements. It is used to draw attention to the element or make it more prominent. The CSS outline properties sets the outline's color, width, and style. Take note that the outline is separate and does not form part of the dimensions of an element.

Outline Style

The outline-style feature is used to style the outline and can have any of these values:

Value	Description
dashed	Sets a dashed outline
dotted	Specifies dotted outline
groove	Used to set 3D grooved outline (The value given for outline-color determines its effect.)
double	Specifies a double outline
Solid	Specifies a solid outline
inset	Used to specify 3D inset outline (The value provided for outline-color determines its effect.)
ridge	Used to set 3D ridged outline (The value provided for outline-color determines its effect.)
outset -	Used to specify 3D outset outline (The value provided for outline-color determines its effect.)
hidden	Sets a hidden outline
none	Sets no outline

Outline Color

The outline-color property is used to set the outline's color.

You can set the color by providing any of the following forms of color values:

name   specifies a color name like "green"
RGB   specifies an RGB value like "rgb(149,0,0)"
Hex   specifies a hex value like "#FFA500"
invert   performs color conversion that displays a visible outline regardless of the background

Outline Width

The outline-width property is used to specify the outline's width. It can be set by applying a predefined value (thin, thick, or medium) or by specifying a size (pt, px, em, cm).

Examples:

p {border: 1px solid gray;}

p.one {
      outline-style: dotted;
      outline-color: green;
      outline-width: medium;
      }

p.two {
      outline-style: dashed;
      outline-color: blue;
      outline-width: 5px;
      }

The following code will illustrate the different outline styles as well as the use of the color and width outline properties. Take note that you have to set the online-style property before the color and width properties can have any effect.

147

```
<!DOCTYPE html>
<html>
  <head>
    <style>
      p {
        border: 2px solid gray;
        outline: 4px color:green;
        }
      p.dashed {outline-style: dashed;}
      p.dotted {outline-style: dotted;}
      p.groove {outline-style: groove;}
      p.double {outline-style: double;}
      p.solid {outline-style: solid;}
      p.inset {outline-style: inset;}
      p.ridge {outline-style: ridge;}
      p.outset {outline-style: outset;}
    </style>
  </head>

  <body>

  <h2>Using outline-style Property</h2>

  <p class="dashed">This is a dashed outline.</p>
  <p class="dotted">This is a dotted outline.</p>
  <p class="groove">This is a grooved outline.</p>
  <p class="double">This is a double outline.</p>
  <p class="solid">This is a solid outline.</p>
  <p class="inset">This is an inset outline.</p>
  <p class="ridge">This is a ridge outline.</p>
  <p class="outset">This is an outset outline.</p>

  </body>
</html>
```

The following figure will show the result when you run the above code:

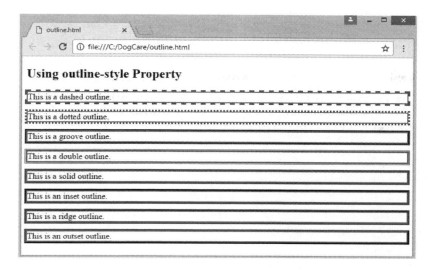

Element Positioning

The position property facilitates the placement of an object or element precisely on a page. You can use any of these four position schemes: absolute, relative, static, and fixed. Elements are positioned using the left, right, top, and bottom properties which will only work if the position party has been set.

Here are the different schemes or methods used in positioning and examples on how to use them:

position: static

HTML elements take the static position by default. Elements that are positioned using this method are not placed in a special way and are unaffected by the left, right, top, and bottom properties. They always follow the normal page flow.

Example:

```
div.static {
    position: static;
    border: 2px solid yellow;
        }
```

position: relative

An element using position:relative is placed relative to its default or normal position. Setting the left, right, top,, and bottom properties will cause the object to move away from its default position. The adjustment may cause a gap but it will prevent other content from filling the gap.

position: fixed

An element using the position:fixed scheme does not move with the scroll action and remains on the same place. You will have to use the right, left, top, and bottom properties to position the object. It doesn't create a gap in the page where it is normally positioned.

For example, take a look at the following code:

```
div.fixed {
    position:fixed;
    bottom:0;
    right:0;
    width:350px;
    border:2px solid blue;
    }
```

position: absolute

An element that uses the position:absolute method is positioned from the defined reference point such as 'from the top' or 'from the right'. It is placed relative to the nearest located ancestor.

For Example:

```
<!DOCTYPE html>
<html>
  <head>
    <style>
      div.relative {
      position: relative;
```

```
    width: 300px;
    height: 150px;
    border: 2px solid gray;
    }

    div.absolute {
    position: absolute;
    top: 70px;
    right: 0;
    width: 220px;
    height: 120px;
    border: 2px solid orange;
    }
  </style>
  </head>
  <body>

  <h3>position: absolute;</h3>

    <p>An element that uses the position:absolute scheme is located relative to
the nearest placed ancestor.

    <div class="relative">This element uses the position:relative;
      <div class="absolute">This element uses the position:absolute;</div>
    </div>

    </body>
</html>
```

The figure below shows the result of the code:

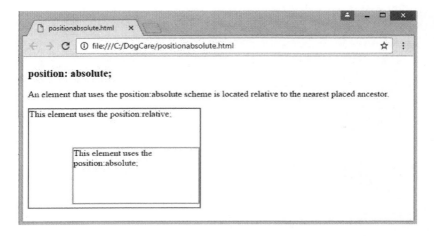

Overlapping Elements

A positioned element can overlap other elements. The z-index property is used to specify an element's stack order and can be positive or negative. The object with greater stack order is placed in front of elements with lower stack order. Take note that when elements with no specified z-index overlap, the last positioned element in the code will be displayed on top.

Example:

```
<!DOCTYPE html>
<html>
 <head>
   <style>
   img {
   position:absolute;
   top: 0px;
    left: 0px;
    z-index: -1;
    }
   </style>
 </head>
 <body>

 <h2>Overlapping Elements</h2>
 <img src="pug.jpeg" width="120" height="130">
 <p>This text overlaps the picture of a pug.</p>

 </body>
</html>
```

Here's how the web page will appear:

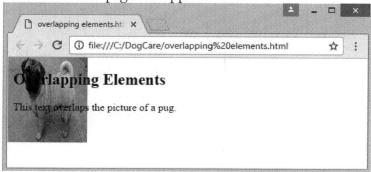

Positioning Text over an Image

To place text over the center of an image, study the following code:

```
<!DOCTYPE html>
<html>
<head>
<style>
.container {
    position:relative;
    }

.center {
    position:absolute;
    top: 50%;
    left: 50%;
    width: 100%
    text-align: center;
    font-size: 30px;
}

img {
    width: 100%;
    height: auto;
}
</style>
</head>
<body>

<h1>Text over Image</h1>
<p>Adding text to the center of an image:</p>

<div class="container">
  <img src="The Alps.jpg" alt="The Alps" width="900" height="280">
  <div class="center">The Alps</div>
</div>

</body>
</html>
```

Here's how the above code will look in Google Chrome:

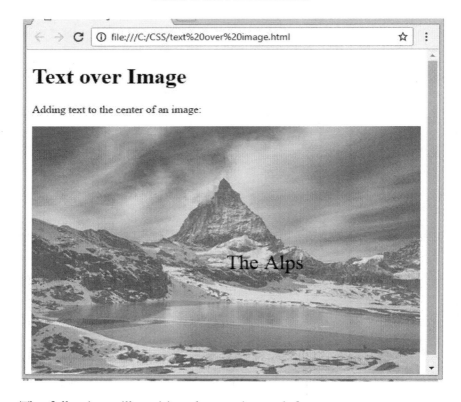

The following will position the text in top left corner:

```
<!DOCTYPE html>
<html>
<head>
<style>
.container {
    position: relative;
            }

.topleft {
    position:absolute;
    top: 10px;
    left: 10px;
    font-size: 32px;


<div class="container">
  <img src="The Alps.jpg" alt="The Alps" width="900" height="280">
```

```
<div class="topleft">The Alps</div>
</div>
```

Here's the result:

Setting the Shape of an Element

An element can be clipped into a specified shape and displayed. The following code will demonstrate how this is done:

```
<!DOCTYPE html>
<html>
  <head>
   <style>
   img {
   position: absolute;
   clip: rect(0px,70px,180px,0px);
      }
   </style>
  </head>
  <body>

   <img src="pug.jpeg" width="120" height="120">

  </body>
  </html>
```

Here's the outcome:

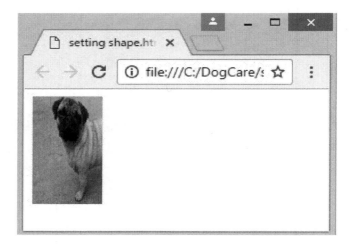

Wrapping Text around an Element

The float property is used to control the location of an element and the location of other elements in relation to it. You can use it to wrap text around an image.

The float property can take one of the following values: left, right, and none.

For example, here's a code that specifies the element to float to the left and for the paragraphs of text to wrap around it:

```
<!DOCTYPE html>
<html>
  <head>
    <style>
      img {
      float: left;
      margin: 10px;
      }
    </style>
  </head>
  <body>

    <p>The image floats to the left of the paragraph and the paragraph content
wraps around the image.</p>

    <p><img src="rose.jpg" alt="rose" width="100" height="140">
    A rose is a woody perennial that typically bears flowers of different shapes
and colors. It is grown in many different parts of the world.
    </body>
</html>
```

This is how the web page will be displayed by browsers:

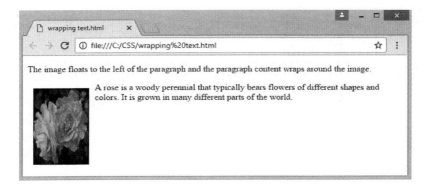

Background

The background properties are used to set the background effects of an element. It allows you to customize a background on web pages, tables, or cells.

The following are the background properties of CSS:

Property	Function	Values
background-color	Specifies the background color	#ff0000
background-image	Sets the background image	url ();
background-repeat	Sets how the background image will be repeated	no-repeat; repeat-x; repeat-y;
background-attachment	Sets whether the background image is fixed or scrolls	fixed; scroll; local; inherit
background-position	Sets the background image's starting position	right top

The background-color property is used to specify an element's background color.

A color is commonly set by any of the following values:

a color name	blue
a HEX notation	#ff0000
an RGB value	rgb(255,0,0)"
an RGB percentage value	rgb(100%, 0, 0)

The following illustrates how the background-color property is used:

```
<!DOCTYPE html>
<html>
 <head>
  <style>
   h1 {
      background-color: #00ff00;
```

```
    }

  div {
     background-color: Bisque;
     }

  p {
     background-color: #7FFF00;
     }
  </style>
</head>
<body>

  <h1>Choosing the Right Shampoo for Your Dog</h1>
  <div>
  Before deciding to buy a shampoo for your dog, you have to consider the
following factors:
     <p>Skin condition</p>
  A moisturing shampoo is indicated if the dog's skin is dry, flaky or itchy.
     <p>Age</p>
  A younger dog typically requires a gentler shampoo.
     </div>
  </body>
</html>
```

The following image shows the effects of using the background-color property:

Background image

The background-image property is used to add an image as a background to the whole web page or element. An image is repeated by default and thus covers the entire page or element.

This property can be set to any of the following values: url ("location"), none, inherit.

The following code illustrates how you can add an image:

```
<!DOCTYPE html>
<html>
 <head>
   <style>
     body {
         background-image:url("sky.jpg");
         }
   </style>
 </head>
 <body>

   <h1>A Clear Day!</h1>

   <p>This page uses a background image.</p>
 </body>
</html>
```

Here's what the code will display:

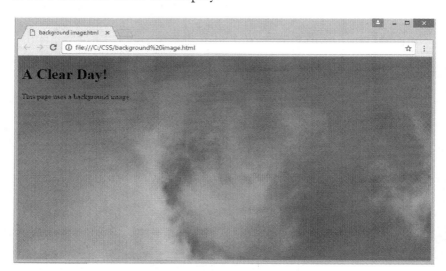

Background-repeat Property

The background-repeat property is used to indicate whether the background image is to be repeated horizontally, vertically, repeated all throughout, not repeated, or not tiled.

Its value may be set to one of the following:

repeat-x	repeats the background horizontally
repeat-y	repeats the background vertically
repeat	default – repeats the background image horizontally and vertically
no repeat	no background repetition
inherit	follow the repeat setting of the parent

By default, the background image is repeated both horizontally and vertically over the entire page. Some images, however, should either be repeated vertically or horizontally or not repeated at all.

For example, this code uses the default repeat value:

```
<!DOCTYPE html>
<html>
  <head>
    <style>
     body {
        background-image: url("plate.jpg");
        }
    </style>
  </head>
  <body>

    <h1>Plates!</h1>
    <p>Confusing background image...</p>

  </body>
</html>
```

This will result to the following web display:

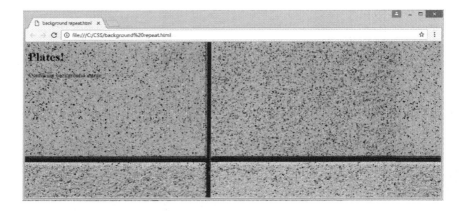

You can set the background-repeat property to 'repeat-y' to prevent the background image from being repeated horizontally:

```
<head>
  <style>
    body {
        background-image: url("plate.jpg");
        background-repeat: repeat-y;
        }
  </style>
</head>
```

The web page will display the following background image:

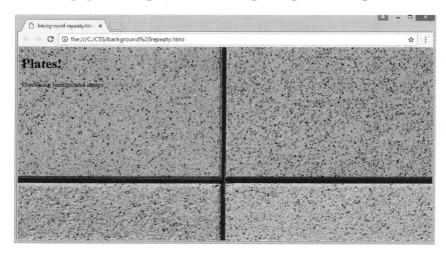

Setting Image Position

An image background may sometimes overpower and disturb the text. The background-position property is used to indicate the placement of the background image. This property can only be used if the image is not tiled.

Background-position can be set to the following values:

top left, top right, center, bottom right, bottom center
value or percentage such as x, y, 90px, 30%

For example, the following code sets the background image to 'no-repeat':

```
<!DOCTYPE html>
<html>
  <head>
    <style>
    body {
        background-image: url("pineapple.jpg");
        background-repeat: no-repeat;
        }
    </style>
  </head>
  <body>

    <h2>Tropical Fruits!</h2>
    <p>Pineapple is one of the many delicious and nutrient-packed tropical
fruits.</p>
    <p>It is a rich source of vitamins and minerals such as Vitamin C,
manganese, copper, and vitamins B6 and B1.

  </body>
</html>
```

This is what the browser will display:

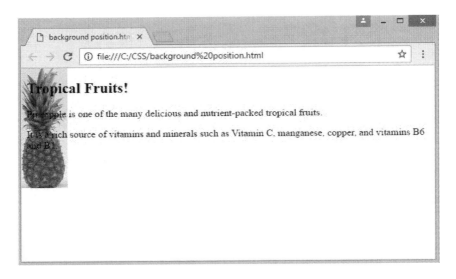

Take note that although the background image is only displayed once, it is interfering with the text. You can solve this by moving the background image to the right. Take a look at the following code:

```
<!DOCTYPE html>
<html>
  <head>
    <style>
    body {
        background-image: url("pineapple.jpg");
        background-repeat: no-repeat;
        background-position: right top;
        margin-right: 220px;
        }

        }
    </style>
  </head>
  <body>

    <h2>Tropical Fruits!</h2>
    <p>Pineapple is one of the many delicious and nutrient-packed tropical fruits.</p>
    <p>It is a rich source of vitamins and minerals such as Vitamin C, manganese, copper, and vitamins B6 and B1.</p>
```

```
</body>
</html>
```

The page will show the following:

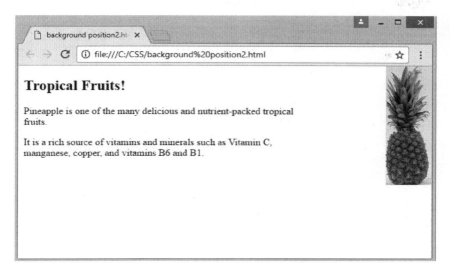

Background-attachment Property

The background-attachment property is used to specify how a background image scrolls with the page. There are three possible values: fixed, scroll, and inherit.

The 'fixed' value sets the background image to a fixed position which does not follow the scroll action.

The 'scroll' value is the default setting and one in which the background scrolls with the page.

The 'inherit' value sets the background to follow the parent's attachment.

The following code will sets the background-attachment to 'fixed':

```
<!DOCTYPE html>
```

165

```
<html>
  <head>
    <style>
      body {
        background-image: url("pineapple.jpg");
        background-position: right top;
        background-repeat: no-repeat;
        background-attachment: fixed;
        margin-right: 220px;
      }
    </style>
  </head>
  <body>

    <h1>Tropical Fruit</h1>
    <p>Pineapple is a tropical fruit. </p>
    <p>Pineapple is a tropical fruit. </p>
    <p>Pineapple is a tropical fruit. </p>
    <p>Pineapple is a tropical fruit. </p>
    <p>Pineapple is a tropical fruit. </p>
    <p>Pineapple is a tropical fruit. </p>
    <p>Pineapple is a tropical fruit. </p>
    <p>Pineapple is a tropical fruit. </p>
    <p>Pineapple is a tropical fruit. </p>
    <p>Pineapple is a tropical fruit. </p>
    <p>Pineapple is a tropical fruit. </p>
    <p>Pineapple is a tropical fruit. </p>
    <p>Pineapple is a tropical fruit. </p>
    <p>Pineapple is a tropical fruit. </p>
    <p>Pineapple is a tropical fruit. </p>
    <p>Pineapple is a tropical fruit. </p>
    <p>Pineapple is a tropical fruit. </p>
    <p>Pineapple is a tropical fruit. </p>
    <p>Pineapple is a tropical fruit. </p>
    <p>Pineapple is a tropical fruit. </p>
    <p>Pineapple is a tropical fruit. </p>

  </body>
</html>
```

The browser will display the background image in a fixed position as the user scrolls through the page:

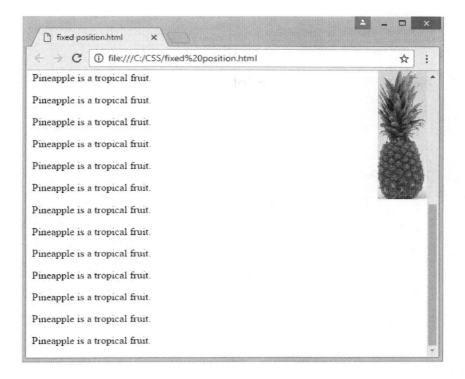

Background - Shorthand property

The background shorthand property can be used to specify more than one or all background properties in one declaration.

When using the background shorthand property, take note that the values should be written in the following order:

- color
- image
- repeat
- attachment
- position

Here is an example of how you can use the background shorthand property inside the <style></style> tags:

167

```
<head>
  <style>
    body {
    background: #ff0000 url("plate.jpg") repeat-x bottom center;
    margin-right: 150px;
    }
  </style>
</head>
```

CSS3 Backgrounds

CSS3 introduced new background properties that provide even greater control over the background element. CSS3 allows the use of multiple background images and now offers the following properties:

- background-origin
- background-size
- background-clip

Multiple Background Images

You can now use the background-image property to add multiple images as background. This is done by separating the background images with a comma. The images will be displayed as stacked images and the first named image is displayed as the closest object to the viewer.

The following code uses two background images:

```
<!DOCTYPE html>
<html>
  <head>
    <style>
      #design1 {
      background-image: url(raspberry.png), url(greenpaper.jpg);
      background-position: right top, left top;
      background-repeat: no-repeat, repeat;
      padding: 15px;
```

```
      }
    </style>
  </head>
  <body>

    <div id="design1">
     <h1>Grandpa's Raspberry Farm</h1>
     <p>Grandpa's Raspberry Farm is where you can find the freshest and best
quality raspberry fruits.</p>
     <p>The farm is open 24/7.</p>
     </div>

  </body>
</html>
```

Here's how the browser will display the web page:

The following demonstrates how to specify multiple images using the background shorthand property:

```
#design1 {
    background: url(raspberry.png) right top no-repeat, url(greenpaper.jpg) left top
repeat;
}
```

Padding

The padding properties let you set the amount of space between the element's content and its borders. It is used to clear the area around the content.

CSS features properties that you can use to set the padding not just for all sides but also for individual sides of an element. The value can be set to a percentage, length, or inherit. An inherit value specifies that an element will take the value of the parent element. A percentage value refers to its percentage in relation to the width of an element's container box. Length sets padding in units such as pt, px, cm, and others.

Setting the Padding for Individual Sides

CSS provides the following attributes for controlling the padding for each side of the element:

padding-bottom   sets an element's bottom padding
padding-top   sets an element's top padding
padding-left   sets an element's left padding
padding-right   sets an element's right padding

This code shows how you can set the individual padding for the different sides of a <p></p> element:

```
p{
  padding-bottom:30px;
  padding-top:20px;
  padding-left:70x;
  padding-right:60px;
  }
```

Padding Shorthand Property

You can shorten the code by specifying one to four values for the four properties using the shorthand property. This single property takes four values as shown in the following example:

```
p{
    padding: 70px 40px 30px 90px;
}
```

Here are the guidelines for applying the supplied values:

If four properties were specified:

padding: 70px 40px 30px 90px;

It is applied as follows:

top padding: 70px
right padding: 40px
bottom padding: 30px
left padding: 90px

If only three values were specified, it is applied as follows:

padding: 70px 60px 55px;

top padding:70px
left and right paddings:50px
bottom padding:55px

If only two values were given, it is applied as follows:

padding: 30px 45px;
bottom and top padding: 30px
left and right padding: 45px

If only one value was specified, it will apply to padding on all sides.

Example:

padding: 75px;

The shorthand property specifies 75px padding for the top, bottom, left, and right sides.

Cursor Property

This property is used to set the cursor style that will be displayed to users. You will often see this property at work when pressing the submit button on a form or when the mouse hovers on a link. For images that don't change in form like submit buttons, the cursor will typically give out a clue that an image can be clicked.

This property can have one of the following values:

default	arrow
pointer	pointing hand
text	"I" bar, indicates that user can select text
auto	cursor shape varies with the context area
crosshair	plus symbol or crosshair
copy	indicates a copy operation
grabbing	indicates that you something is available for grabbing
move	'I' image
n-resize	indicates movement of the edge upwards or towards the north
e-resize	indicates movement of the edge towards the east (right)
s-resize	indicates movement of the edge downwards or towards the south
w-resize	indicates movement of the edge to the west (left)
ne-resize	indicates movement of the edge upward towards the right (north east)
se-resize	indicates movement of the edge downwards towards the right (south east)
nw-resize	indicates movement of the edge upwards towards the left (north west)
sw-resize	indicates movement of the edge downwards towards the left (south west)
nesw-resize	indicates cursor resize in two directions
no-drop	indicate an area where a grabbed item could not be dropped

none	indicates that no cursor is assigned to an element
wait	hourglass
cell	indicates that a user can select a cell or group of cells
progress	indicates an ongoing process
all-scroll	indicates that you can scroll in different directions
context-menu	indicates availability of context menu
col-resize	indicates that the user can horizontally resize a column
row-resize	indicates that a user can vertically resize a row
help	balloon or question mark
<url>	cursor image source
zoom-in	indicates an area that a user can zoom in
zoom-out	indicates an area that a user can zoom out
inherit	specifies that the values will be inherited from the parent element
alias	indicates that an alias will be created

Example:

```
<body>
  <p>Watch the cursor change as you move the mouse:</p>
    <div style="cursor:pointer">pointer</div>
    <div style="cursor:wait">Wait</div>
    <div style="cursor:text">Text</div>
    <div style="cursor:help">Help</div>
</body>
```

CHAPTER 17: STYLING BORDERS

Adding a Border

The border property is used to add a border to a webpage. This property lets you specify the thickness value to thin, medium, or thick. You can also use border styles such as solid, groove, ridge, double, inset, outset, dashed, or dotted.

To illustrate, create a new style file and save it as style8.css:

```
p {
  border: thick inset;
  }
```

Link the new css file to the html file:

```
<head>
   <title>Dog Breeds</title>
      <link rel="stylesheet" href="style/fontstyle3.css" type="text/css"/>
      <link rel="stylesheet" href="style/style7.css" type="text/css"/>
      <link rel="stylesheet" href="style/style8.css" type="text/css"/>
</head>
<body>
      <h3 align="center"> Popular Dog Breeds </h3>
      <p text-align="justify">The Shih Tzu is a strong and sturdy toy dog with a sweet-natured temperament. The Bulldog is a sturdy medium-sized dog with a wrinkled mug and a distinctive underbite. The Yorkshire Terrier is a tiny dog with an inquisitive temperament and stunning coat.</p>
</body>
```

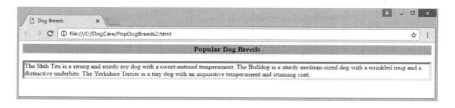

174

Border Design

The CSS border-style defines the type of border that will be displayed. It can have one to four (for the top, bottom, right, and left border) of these values:

Value	Function
dashed	To set dashed borders
dotted	To set dotted borders
groove	To set 3D grooved borders. (The outline-color value determines its effect)
solid	To specify solid borders
double	To specify double borders
inset	To specify 3D inset borders (The outline-color value determines its effect.)
ridge	To set 3D ridged borders (The outline-color value determines its effect.)
outset -	To specify 3D outset borders (The outline-color value determines its effect)
hidden	To set hidden borders
none	To set no border

The following code will demonstrate how you can use the border-style feature:

```
<!DOCTYPE html>
<html>
  <head>
    <style>
      p.dotted {border-style:dotted;}
      p.groove {border-style:groove;}
      p.solid {border-style:solid;}
      p.inset {border-style:inset;}
      p.ridge {border-style:ridge;}
      p.dashed {border-style:dashed;}
      p.double {border-style:double;}
      p.hidden {border-style:hidden;}
      p.outset {border-style:outset;}
      p.mix {border-style:dashed dotted double solid;}
    </style>
  </head>
  <body>
    <h1>CSS border-style Property</h1>
    <p>The border-style property sets the type of border that will be
displayed:</p>
    <p class="dashed">Dashed border</p>
    <p class="dotted">Dotted border</p>
    <p class="groove">Grooved border</p>
    <p class="solid">Solid border</p>
    <p class="double">Double border</p>
    <p class="inset">Inset border</p>
    <p class="ridge">Ridge border</p>
    <p class="outset">Outset border</p>
    <p class="hidden">Hidden border</p>
    <p class="mix">Mixed border</p>
  </body>
</html>
```

The image below shows the application of the different border styles:

CSS border-style Property

The border-style property sets the type of border that will be displayed:

```
┌ ─ ─ ─ ─ ─ ─ ─ ─ ─ ─ ─ ─ ─ ─ ─ ─ ─ ─ ─ ─ ─ ┐
│Dashed border                               │
└ ─ ─ ─ ─ ─ ─ ─ ─ ─ ─ ─ ─ ─ ─ ─ ─ ─ ─ ─ ─ ─ ┘
```

```
..............................................
:Dotted border                               :
..............................................
```

```
┌────────────────────────────────────────────┐
│Groove border                                │
└────────────────────────────────────────────┘
```

```
┌────────────────────────────────────────────┐
│Solid border                                 │
└────────────────────────────────────────────┘
```

```
┌────────────────────────────────────────────┐
│Double border                                │
└────────────────────────────────────────────┘
```

```
┌────────────────────────────────────────────┐
│Inset border                                 │
└────────────────────────────────────────────┘
```

```
┌────────────────────────────────────────────┐
│Ridge border                                 │
└────────────────────────────────────────────┘
```

```
┌────────────────────────────────────────────┐
│Outset border                                │
└────────────────────────────────────────────┘
```

Hidden border

No border

```
┌ ─ ─ ─ ─ ─ ─ ─ ─ ─ ─ ─ ─ ─ ─ ─ ─ ─ ─ ─ ─ ─ ┐
│Mixed border                                 :
└ ─ ─ ─ ─ ─ ─ ─ ─ ─ ─ ─ ─ ─ ─ ─ ─ ─ ─ ─ ─ ─ ┘
```

Take note you need to set the border-style before other border properties such as border-width and border-color can have any effect on the element.

Setting the Borders' Width

The border-width attribute is used to specify the borders' width. You can set the width to any of these values:

specific size: cm, px, em, pt
predefined value: think, thick, medium

This property can take 1 to 4 values to set the right, left, bottom, and top borders.

The code below illustrates how to set the border-width:

```
<!DOCTYPE html>
<html>
  <head>
    <style>
        p.border1 {
        border-style: dashed;
        border-width: medium;
        }

        p.border2 {
        border-style: solid;
        border-width: 10px;
        }

        p.border3 {
        border-style: double;
        border-width: 5px;
        }

        p.border4 {
        border-style: solid;
        border-width: thin;
        }

        p.border5 {
        border-style: dashed;
        border-width: 15px;
        }
```

```
      p.border6 {
      border-style: ridge;
      border-width: thick;
      }

      p.border7 {
      border-style:dashed dotted double solid;
      border-width: 2px 10px 4px 20px;
      }
    </style>
  </head>
  <body>

  <h1>CSS border-width Property</h1>
  <p>The border-width property sets the width of an element's borders:</p>

  <p class="border1">Dashed border</p>
  <p class="border2">Solid border</p>
  <p class="border3">Double border</p>
  <p class="border4">Solid border</p>
  <p class="border5">Dashed border</p>
  <p class="border6">Ridge border</p>
  <p class="border7">Mixed border</p>

  </body>
</html>
```

This image shows the effects the width setting on the borders:

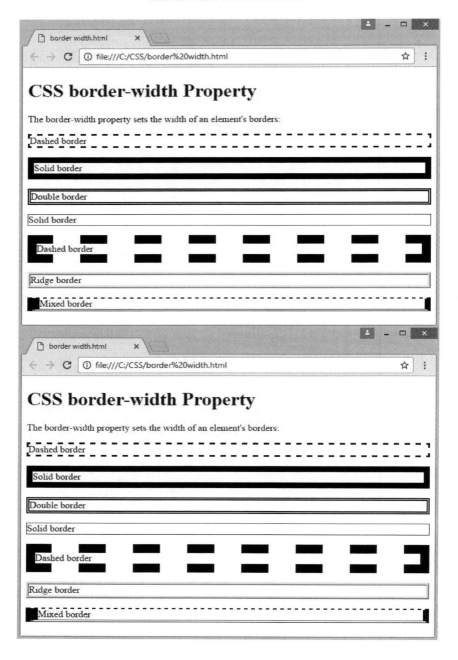

Border Colors

The border-color feature enables users to specify the borders' colors.

It can take any of these color values:

color name   "red"
Hex   "#ff0000"
RGB   "rgb(250,0,0)"

It can take as many as 4 values to set the top, bottom, right, and left borders.

When not set, the borders inherit the element's color.

The following code illustrates how the border-color property is set:

```
<!DOCTYPE html>
<html>
  <head>
    <style>
      p.border1 {
      border-style: double;
      border-color: green;
      }

      p.border2 {
      border-style: solid;
      border-color: blue green red yellow;
      }

      p.border3 {
      border-style: dotted;
      border-color: yellow;
      }
    </style>
  </head>
  <body>

    <h1>CSS border-color Property</h1>
    <p>The border-color property is used to set the color of the borders.:</p>

    <p class="border1">Double green borders</p>
    <p class="border2">Solid multicolor borders</p>
    <p class="border3">Dotted yellow borders</p>

  </body>
</html>
```

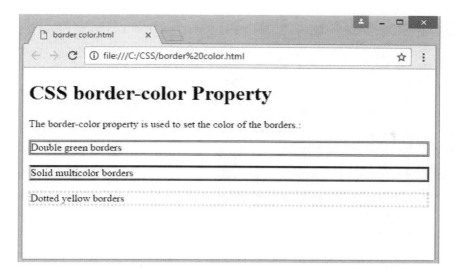

Borders - Individual Sides

CSS lets you set a different style for the right, left, top, and bottom borders.

You can provide as many as four values. The following rules will determine how the values will be applied:

If you specify one value for the border-style property:

Example:

border-style: double;

The four borders will have double style.

If you specify two values for the border-color property:

border-style: solid dashed

The top and bottom borders will be solid while the left and right borders will be dashed.

If you set three values for the borders:

border-style: dashed, double, solid

The top border will be dashed, the left and right borders will be double, and the bottom border will be solid.

If you specify four values for the borders:

Ex. border-style: dashed double dotted solid

The top border will be dashed, the right border will be double, the bottom border will be dotted, and the left border will be solid.

You can also style the border-width and border-color individually for each side.

Border Shorthand Property

You can shorten the CSS code and specify all border properties using the border shorthand property.

The border property lets you use specify the following individual properties with a single property:

- border-style
- border-width
- border-color

The code below demonstrates how you can use the border shorthand property:

```
<!DOCTYPE html>
<html>
  <head>
    <style>
      p {
        border: 10px double green;
        }
```

```
    </style>
  </head>
  <body>

    <h2>The Border Shorthand Property</h2>

      <p>The border shorthand property is used to specify border-style, border-width, and border-color in one declaration.</p>

    </body>
</html>
```

This image shows what the code does:

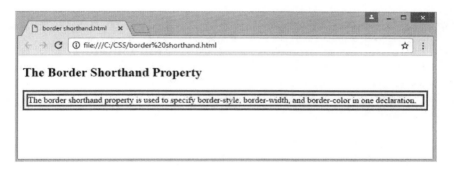

Rounded Corners

The border-radius property is used to give an element the "rounded corners' design.

Rules for Specifying Corners

If only one value is specified for the border-radius property, this value will apply to all four corners.

You can, however, specify a radius for each corner. Following are the rules for applying the radius:

Two values:

The first value applies to the bottom-right and top-left corner while the second value applies to the bottom-left and top-right corner.

Three values:

The first values to the top-left corner, the second value applies to the top-right, and the third value applies to the bottom-right corner.

Four values:

The values apply according to the following sequence: top-left then top-right then bottom-right then bottom-left corner.

Following are examples that demonstrate how the border-radius property is used:

```
<!DOCTYPE html>
<html>
<head>
<style>
#corners1 {
    border-radius: 30px;
    background: yellow;
    padding: 20px;
    width: 220px;
    height: 200px;
}

#corners2 {
    border-radius: 15px 50px;
    border: 2px solid yellow;
    padding: 15px;
    width: 220px;
    height: 200px;
}

#corners3 {
    border-radius: 15px 50px 30px;
    background: url(greenpaper.jpg);
    background-repeat: repeat;
    background-position: left top;
    padding: 15px;
    width: 220px;
    height: 200px;
}
```

```
#corners4 {
    border-radius: 15px 50px 30px 10px;
    border: 2px solid green;
    padding: 15px;
    width: 220px;
    height: 200px;
}


</style>
</head>
<body>

<p>The border-radius property is used to add rounded corners.<p>
<p>Four equally rounded corners for an object with a background color:</p>
<p id="corners1">Figure 1</p>
<p>Rounded corners for an object with border:</p>
<p id="corners2">Figure 2</p>
<p>Rounded corners for an object with background image:</p>
<p id="corners3">Figure 3</p>
<p>Four unequally rounded corners for an object:</p>
<p id="corners4">Figure 4</p>

</body>
</html>
```

The browser will display the borders as follows:

The border-radius property is used to add rounded corners

Four equally rounded corners for an object with a background color:

Rounded corners for an object with border:

Rounded corners for an object with background image:

Four unequally rounded corners for an object:

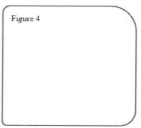

Border Image

Border-image, a CSS3 feature, allows you to use an image as a border.

It has the following parts:

- The image that will be used as a border
- A statement specifying where the image will be sliced

188

- A definition whether the middle sections will be stretched or repeated

For this feature to take effect, you have to set the border property first.

Here are some of the values that you can set if you want to use an image for borders:

To define image path, you will use the border-image-source.

Example: border-image-source: url(banner.jpg);

To set the width of the image, you can use the border-image-width. Example: border-image-width:25px;

To slice the image, you will use border-image-slice.

Example: border-image-slice: 30;

To specify whether you want the image to be stretched, rounded, or repeated, you will use the border-image-repeat.

Example: border-image-repeat: round;

This code demonstrates how the image border is set:

```html
<html>
  <head>

    <style>
      #borderimage1 {
        border: 10px solid transparent;
        padding: 15px;
        border-image-source: url(banner.jpg);
        border-image-width: 15px;
          border-image-repeat: round;
        border-image-slice: 30;
        }
      #borderimage2 {
        border: 10px solid transparent;
        padding: 15px;
        border-image-source: url(banner.jpg);
        border-image-width: 20px;
        border-image-repeat: round;
        border-image-slice: 30;
        }
      #borderimage3 {
        border: 10px solid transparent;
        padding: 15px;
        border-image-source: url(banner.jpg);
        border-image-width: 25px;
        border-image-repeat: round;
        border-image-slice: 30;
        }
    </style>

  </head>
  <body>
    <p id="borderimage1">An image border</p>
    <p id="borderimage2">An image border</p>
    <p id="borderimage3">An image border</p>
    <p>Here's the original image:</p><img src="banner.jpg">
  </body>
</html>
```

This shows how the browser will display the image borders:

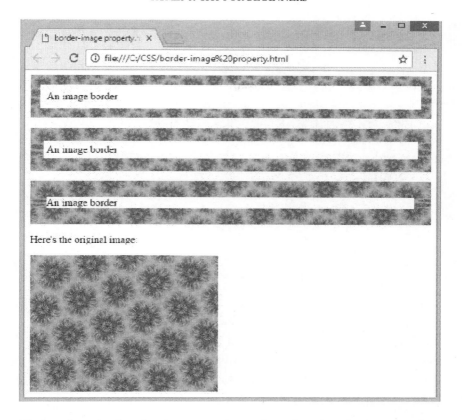

Notice that the border-image property is a shorthand property that allows you to declare the source, image width, slice, outset, and repeat properties in one declaration.

CHAPTER 18: STYLING LISTS

In your HTML lessons, you have learned that you can style unordered lists with bullets and ordered lists with numbers or letters. Using CSS, you can apply other styles such as images or drawn objects. You will use the list-style property to specify the list item marker.

List Properties

Following are the CSS list properties:

Property	Function
list-style-type	Specifies the list-item marker
list-style-position	Indicates the position (inside or outside) of the list item marker
list-style-image	Specifies the image to be used as a list item marker
list-style	Shorthand property for list in one declaration

List-style-type property

The list-style-type property sets what type of list bullet will be used. There are several types of bullets to choose from:

disc	round bullets
square	square bullets
circle	circular bullets
lower-roman	Roman numeral in lowercase
upper-roman	Roman numeral in uppercase
lower-alpha	alphabet lowercase
upper-alpha	alphabet uppercase
decimal	regular numbering
decimal-leading-zero	regular numbering with leading zeroes

The following codes show how you can style lists in CSS:

ul.a {list-style-type: disc;}
ul.b {list-style-stype:upper-roman;}
ol.a {list-style-type:square;}
ol.b {list-style-type:lower-alpha;}

List-style-image property

The list-style-image property is used to set an image for use as a list marker.

Here is an example of code where an image is used as a list bullet:

```
ul {
    list-style-image:url ( 'dog1.gif');
    }
```

List-style-type property

You can use the shorthand property to specify all list properties in a single declaration. Take note that you have to observe the following order of values:

- list-style-type
- list-style-position
- list-style-image

Example:

```
ul {
    list-style: circle inside url("dog1.gif");
    }
```

The following illustrates how a list is designed in CSS:

193

Create a css file and save it as liststye.css:

```
.DecimalLeadingOrdered {
   list-style-type: decimal-leading-zero;
   font-family: Georgia, Verdana;
   font-size: 20px }

.InsideImage {
   list-style-image:
   url(sampleCSSListBulletImage.jpg);
   list-style-position: inside;
   font-family: Verdana, Times;
   font-size: 22px }
```

Link the liststyle.css to the HTML document:

```
<head>
   <title>Spark Ignition</title>
      <link rel="stylesheet" href="style/liststyle.css" type="text/css">
</head>
<body>

   <h1>Spark Ignition System:</h1>

   <ol class=DecimalLeadingOrdered>
   <li>battery</li>
   <li>ignition switch</li>
   <li>resistor</li>
   <li>ignition coil</li>
   <li>condenser</li>
   <li>capacitor</li>
   </ol>
   <br>

   <ul class="InsideImage">
   <li>ignition coil</li>
   <li>distributor cap</li>
   <li>rotor</li>
   <li>spark plug</li>
   </ul>
   </body>
</html>
```

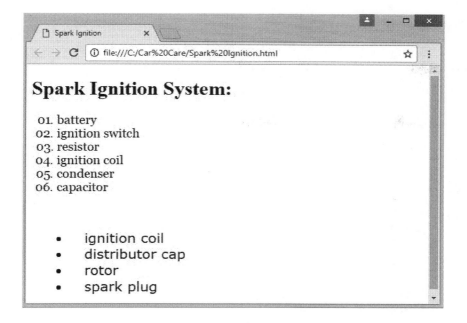

Styling List with Colors

You can style lists with colors to make them more interesting.

Adding a style within the <ol></ol) or <ul></ul> tag will affect the entire list while adding properties to the <li></li> tag will affect each list item.

Example:

```
<!DOCTYPE html>
 <html>
  <head>
   <style>
    ol {
       background:#ffebcd;
       padding:15px;
       }

    ul {
       background:#deb887;
```

```
        padding:15px;
        }

    ol li {
        background: #5f9ea0;
        padding:5px;
        margin-left:25px;
        }

    ul li {
        background:#7b68ee;
        margin: 5px;
        }
    </style>
</head>
<body>

<h1>Spark Ignition System:</h1>

<ol>
<li>battery</li>
<li>ignition switch</li>
<li>resistor</li>
<li>ignition coil</li>
<li>condenser</li>
<li>capacitor</li>
</ol>

<ul>
<li>ignition coil</li>
<li>distributor cap</li>
<li>rotor</li>
<li>spark plug</li>
</ul>

</body>
</html>
```

This is how the web page will appear:

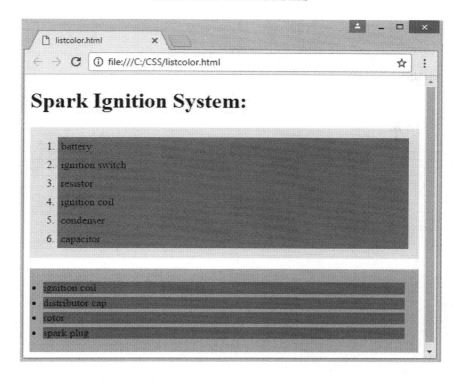

CHAPTER 19: OTHER CSS3 FEATURES

Pseudo-elements

Pseudo-elements are used to style a specific part or several parts of HTML elements. They let you add special effects to a few selectors.

The following are the most commonly used pseudo-elements:

Value	Description
:first-line	Used to add special styles to the first line of a text
:first-letter	Used to add special style to the first letter of a text
:before	Used to insert content before an element
:after	Used to add content after an element

The :first letter pseudo-element

The properties that may be applied to the first-letter pseudo-element include font, color, margin, padding, border, background,, vertical-align, text-decoration, text-transform, float, clear, and line-height.

Example:

```
p:first-letter {
   color:blue;
   font-size:x-large;
```

The :first line pseudo-element

The properties that may be applied to the first-line pseudo-element include font, color, text-decoration, text-transform, vertical-align, letter-spacing, word-spacing, clear, and line-height.

```
p:first-line {
   text-decoration: underline
   color:#ff0000;
   font-variant:small-caps;
   }
```

CSS3 Colors

As you have learned in earlier sections, CSS allows you to use color names, RGB and hexadecimal colors.

CSS3 now supports the following:

- RGBA colors
- HSL colors
- HSLA colors
- opacity

RGBA Color Values

RGBA stands for Red Green Blue Alpha. It extends the RGB color with an alpha channel which sets the color opacity between 0.0 and 1.0 (from fully transparent to fully opaque).

The following code shows examples of color setting using RGBA:

```
<head>
```

```
<style>
#par1{background-color: rgba(255, 0, 0, 0.3)}
#par2{background-color: rgba(0, 255, 0, 0.3);}
#par3{background-color: rgba(0, 0, 255, 0.3);}
</style>
</head>
```

HSL Colors

HSL means Hue, Saturation, and Lightness.

You can set an HSL value with this syntax:

hsl(hue, saturation, lightness)

Hue   a degree on the color wheel (0 to 360)
Saturation   percentage where full color is set as 100%
Lightness   percentage where black is 0% and white is 100%

These examples illustrate how HSL color is set:

```
#par1 {background-color: hsl(150, 100%, 60%);}
#par2 {background-color: hsl(120, 85%, 20%);}
#par3 {background-color: hsl(100, 90%, 20%);}
#par4 {background-color: hsl(120, 70%, 50%);}
```

HSLA Colors

HSLA colors extend the HSL colors with an alpha channel which sets the color opacity between 0.00 (fully transparent) and 1.0 (fully opaque).

The following shows how you can specify HSLA colors:

```
#par1 {background-color: hsla(150, 100%, 75%, 0.5);}
#par2 {background-color: hsla(120, 75%, 50%, 0.5);}
#par3 {background-color: hsla(150, 100%, 75%, 0.6);}
#par4 {background-color: hsla(120, 75%, 50%, 0.4);}
```

Opacity

The opacity property defines the opacity for the entire element. This means that both text and background color will be opaque or transparent. The value must be between 0.00 to indicate fully transparent to 1.0 to indicate fully opaque.

To set red with opacity:

#par1 {background-color:rgb(255,0,0);opacity:0.6;}

To set green with opacity:

#par2 {background-color:rgb(0,255,0);opacity:0.6;}

To set blue with opacity:

#par3 {background-color:rgb(0,0,255);opacity:0.6;}

Gradients

The gradients feature introduced in CSS3 facilitates smooth transitions when using a combination of different colors. The use of gradients can lessen download time significantly and produce better zoomed images. They are commonly used as background images.

CSS3 features the following gradients:

- Linear Gradients (goes up/down/right/left/diagonally)
- Radial Gradients (appears at the center)

While most browsers have eliminated the need for a prefix when setting the gradients, it is still a good practice to include them to ensure that your web page will get full support.

Here are the prefixes for the different browsers:

Safari 5.1 to 6.0   -webkit-linear-gradient
Opera 11.1 to 12.0   -o-linear-gradient
Firefox 3.6 to 15   -moz-linear-gradient

The standard syntax is used for most modern browsers and it should be placed last. Take note that Internet Explorer 9 and its earlier versions do not support gradients.

CSS3 Linear Gradients

Linear gradients refer to the arrangement of at least two colors in a linear format (left to right, top to bottom). To create linear gradients, you have to set at least two colors as color stops. You may also define a starting point and direction with the gradient effect.

Here is the syntax for setting linear gradients:

background: linear-gradient(color1, color2, ...);

Examples:

Top to Bottom Linear Gradient(default)

```
<!DOCTYPE html>
<html>
  <head>
    <style>
      #grad1 {
        height: 220px;
        background: green;
        background: -webkit-linear-gradient(green, red);
        background: -o-linear-gradient(green, red);
        background: -moz-linear-gradient(green, red);
        background: linear-gradient(green, red);
        }
    </style>
  </head>
```

```
<body>
  <h1>Top to Bottom Linear Gradient</h1>
  <p>This is a linear gradient that starts at green and transitions to red./p>
  <div id="grad1"></div>
</body>
```

This image shows the top to bottom linear gradient:

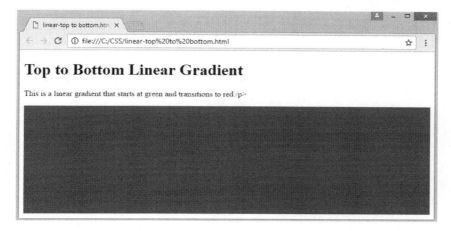

Left to Right Linear Gradient

The following code sets a linear gradient from left to right starting at green and transitioning to red:

```
<!DOCTYPE html>
<html>
  <head>
    <style>
      #gradtwo {
            height: 220px;
            background: green;
            background: -webkit-linear-gradient(green, red);
            background: -o-linear-gradient(right, green, red);
            background: -moz-linear-gradient(right, green, red);
            background: linear-gradient(to right, green, red);
            }
    </style>
  </head>
  <body>

    <h1>Left to Right Linear Gradient</h1>
    <p>This is a linear gradient that starts green at the left and transitions to
red:</p>

    <div id="gradtwo"></div>
  </body>
```

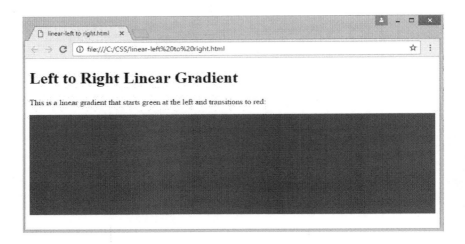

Diagonal Linear Gradient

You can create a diagonal gradient by defining both vertical and horizontal starting positions.

Example:

```
<!DOCTYPE html>
<html>
  <head>
    <style>
      #grad3 {
            height: 220px;
            background: green;
            background: -webkit-linear-gradient(left top, green, red);
            background: -o-linear-gradient(bottom right, green, red);
            background: -moz-linear-gradient(bottom right, green, red);
            background: linear-gradient(to bottom right, green, red);
            }
    </style>
  </head>




  <body>
    <h1>Diagonal Linear Gradient</h1>
    <p>This diagonal gradient starts at green and transitions to red:</p>
    <div id="grad3"></div>
  </body>
```

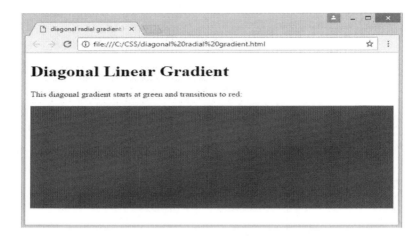

Defining Angles

The use of angles gives you more control over the gradient's direction than when using one of the predefined directions like top to bottom.

Here's the syntax:

background: linear-gradient(angle, color1, color2);

The angle refers to the specified angle between a horizontal and gradient line.

The following code demonstrates the effect of using different angles on linear gradients:

```
<!DOCTYPE html>
<html>
  <head>
    <style>
      #gradang1 {
         height: 120px;
         background: green;
         background: linear-gradient(0deg, green, red);
         }
      #gradang2 {
         height: 120px;
         background: green;
         background: linear-gradient(90deg, green, red);
         }
      #gradang3 {
         height: 120px;
         background: green;
         background: linear-gradient(-90deg, green, red);
         }
      #gradang4 {
         height: 120px;
         background: green;
         background: linear-gradient(180deg, green, red);
         }
    </style>
  </head>
<body>
<h1>Linear Gradients with Angles</h1>
<div id="gradang1" style="color:yellow;text-align:center;">0deg</div><br>
<div id="gradang2" style="color:yellow;text-align:center;">90deg</div><br>
<div id="gradang3" style="color:yellow;text-align:center;">-90deg</div><br>
<div id="gradang4" style="color:yellow;text-align:center;">180deg</div>
</body>
</html>
```

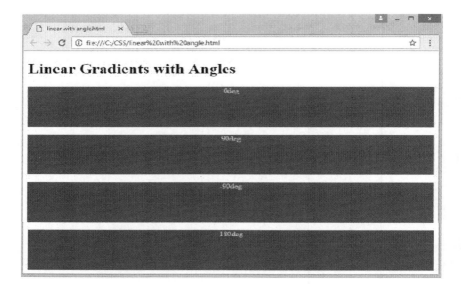

Linear Gradient with Multiple Colors

You can specify a linear gradient with multiple colors.

Here's a code that uses several colors for a linear gradient:

```
<!DOCTYPE html>
<html>
<head>
<style>
#gra1 {
    height: 60px;
    background: -webkit-linear-gradient(left, green, yellow, red, blue, orange, violet, indigo);
    background: -o-linear-gradient(left, green, yellow, red, blue, orange, violet, indigo);
    background: -moz-linear-gradient(left, green, yellow, red, blue, orange, violet, indigo);
    background: linear-gradient(to right, green, yellow, red, blue, orange, violet, indigo);
}
</style>
</head>
<body>

<div id="gra1" style="text-align:center;margin:auto;color:white;font-size:45px;font-weight:bold">
Multiple Colors Gradient Background
</div>

</body>
</html>
```

208

Transparency

CSS3 supports transparency which you can use to create fading effects.

To use this feature, you will have to use the rgba() function to specify the color stops and provide a parameter to define the transparency. The value can be a number from 0 (full transparency) to 1 (no transparency).

This code displays a linear gradient from left to right that starts fully transparent and transitions to green.

```
<!DOCTYPE html>
<html>
<head>
<style>
#gra1 {
    height: 180px;
    background: -webkit-linear-gradient(left, rgba(0,255,0,0), rgba(0,255,0,3));
    background: -o-linear-gradient(right, rgba(0,255,0,0), rgba(0,255,0,3));
    background: -moz-linear-gradient(right, rgba(0,255,0,0), rgba(0,255,0,3));
    background: linear-gradient(to right, rgba(0,255,0,0), rgba(0,255,0,3));
}
</style>
</head>
<body>

<h1>Linear Gradient Transparency</h1>
<p>The rgba() function is used to define the color stops and to add transparency.</p>

<div id="gra1"></div>

</body>
</html>
```

209

This figure shows the result of adding transparency to gradients:

Repeating Linear Gradients

CSS3 allows you to repeat a linear gradient with the function repeating-linear-gradient().

This code shows how you can use this function to repeat linear gradients:

```
<!DOCTYPE html>
<html>
  <head>
    <style>
      #gradone {
        height: 250px;
        background: -webkit-repeating-linear-gradient(yellow, green 10%, red 20%);
        background: -o-repeating-linear-gradient(yellow, green 10%, red 20%);
        background: -moz-repeating-linear-gradient(yellow, green 10%, red 20%);
        background: repeating-linear-gradient(yellow, green 10%, red 20%);
        }
    </style>
  </head>
  <body>
    <h1>Repeating Linear Gradient</h1>
    <div id="gradone"></div>
  </body>
</html>
```

Your browser will show the following:

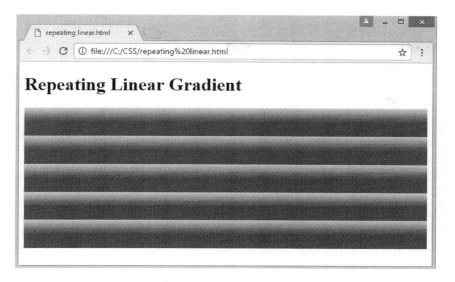

Radial Gradients

A radial gradient appears at the center. To create radial gradients, you have to specify at least two color stops.

Here's a code that shows how you can create a radial gradient:

```
<!DOCTYPE html>
<html>
  <head>
    <style>
      #gra1 {
          height: 200px;
          width: 220px;
          background: yellow;
          background: -webkit-radial-gradient(yellow, green, blue);
          background: -o-radial-gradient(yellow, green, blue);
          background: -moz-radial-gradient(yellow, green, blue);
          background: radial-gradient(yellow, green, blue);
          }
    </style>
  </head>
  <body>

  <h1>Radial Gradient with Evenly Spaced Color Stops</h1>
  <div id="gra1"></div>

  </body>
</html>
```

The code will output a gradient with evenly spaced color stops:

Repeating Radial Gradients

To repeat radial gradients, you can use the repeating-radial-gradient() function.

Here's an example:

```
<!DOCTYPE html>
<html>
<head>
<style>
#radgrad {
    height: 200px;
    width: 250px;
    background: -webkit-repeating-radial-gradient(yellow, green 7%, red 10%);
    background: -o-repeating-radial-gradient(yellow, green 7%, red 10%);
    background: -moz-repeating-radial-gradient(yellow, green 7%, red 10%);
    background: repeating-radial-gradient(yellow, green 7%, red 10%);
}
</style>
</head>
<body>

<h3>A Repeating Radial Gradient</h3>

<div id="radgrad"></div>

</body>
</html>
```

This is what you'll get:

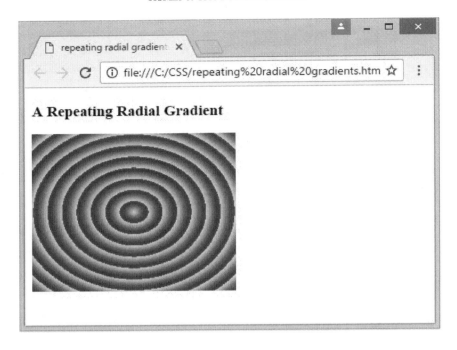

Setting the Size of Gradients

The size parameter is used to define the size of a gradient. Its value can be any of the following:

- closest-side
- closest-corner
- farthest-side
- farthest-corner (default)

This example will demonstrate how the size parameter is used to set the size of a radial gradient:

```html
<!DOCTYPE html>
<html>
<head>
<style>
   #radgrad1 {
   height: 120px;
   width: 120px;
   background: radial-gradient(closest-side at 50% 45%, orange, green, blue); /
}
#radgrad2 {
   height: 120px;
   width: 120px;
   background: radial-gradient(closest-corner at 50% 45%, orange, green, blue);
   }
#radgrad3 {
   height: 120px;
   width: 120px;
   background: radial-gradient(farthest-side at 50% 45%, orange, green, blue);
   }
#radgrad4 {
   height: 120px;
   width: 120px;
   background: radial-gradient(farthest-corner at 50% 45%, orange, green, blue);
   }
</style>
</head>
<body>

<h2>Radial Gradients Sizes</h2>

<p><strong>closest-side</strong></p>
<div id="radgrad1"></div>

<p><strong>closest-corner</strong></p>
<div id="radgrad2"></div>

<p><strong>farthest-side</strong></p>
<div id="radgrad3"></div>

<p><strong>farthest-corner</strong></p>
<div id="radgrad4"></div>

</body>
</html>
```

The following images show the results of the code:

closest-side

closest-corner

farthest-side

farthest-corner

Shadow Effects

CSS3 lets you add shadow effects to text and element with the text-shadow and box-shadow elements.

Text Shadow

The text-shadow property is used to apply shadow to text. To use, you only need to set both the horizontal shadow and vertical shadow.

For example:

```
h2 {
   text-shadow: 2px 2px;
   }
```

You can add color to the shadow by including a color.

This code displays text with green shadows:

```
<!DOCTYPE html>
<html>
  <head>
    <style>
    h2 {
    text-shadow: 2px 2px green;
    }
    </style>
  </head>
  <body>

  <h2>Cute Dogs</h2>

  </body>
</html>
```

Here's the result:

You can also use a blur effect with this code:

```
h2 {
  text-shadow: 2px 2px 7px green;
  }
```

You can set a white text with black shadow with this code:

```
h2 {
  color: white;
  text-shadow: 2px 2px 7px black;
  }
```

Here's what the browser will display:

Multiple Shadows

To specify multiple shadows to a text, you will simply specify each shadow and separate the shadow definitions with a comma.

For example, the following code adds gold and green shadows to the text:

```
<!DOCTYPE html>
<html>
  <head>
    <style>
      h2 {
        text-shadow: 0 0 7px #FFD700, 0 0 5px green;
        }


    </style>
  </head>
  <body>

    <h2>Cute Dogs!</h2>

</body>
</html>
```

This image shows the combination of the two shadows:

219

Border around Text

The text-shadow property can be used to create a border around the text.

```
<!DOCTYPE html>
<html>
  <head>
    <style>
      h2 {
        color: green;
        text-shadow: -1px 0 red, 0 1px red, 1px 0 red, 0 -1px red;
        }
    </style>
  </head>
  <body>

    <h2>Cute Dogs</h2>

  </body>
</html>
```

220

The box-shadow Property

The box-shadow property is used to apply shadow to an element.

To use it, you have to set at least the horizontal and vertical shadow with a code like this:

```
<!DOCTYPE html>
<html>
  <head>
    <style>
     div {
       width: 200x;
       height: 75px;
       padding: 12px;
       background-color: grey;
       box-shadow: 12px 12px;
     }
    </style>
  </head>
  <body>

    <div>Box Shadow</div>

  </body>
</html>
```

Your browser will display the following box with shadows:

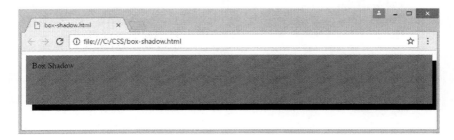

The default shadow color is black but you can set it to another color by adding a color parameter. Here's an example:

```
div {
    box-shadow: 12px 12px green;
```

221

}

This is how the box shadow will look:

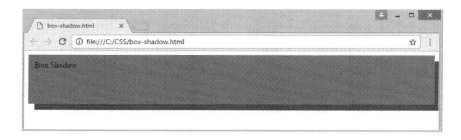

You can also add a blur effect to the box shadow:

div {
    box-shadow: 12px 12px 6px green;
    }

This is a box with a blur effect:

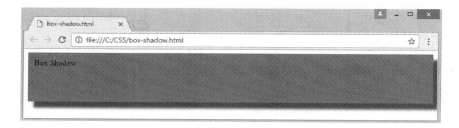

2D Transforms

A transformation effect allows an element to change its position, size, and shape.

CSS3 supports 2d and 3d transformation effects which let you rotate, translate, skew, and scale elements.

222

CSS3 features several 2D transformation methods:

- translate()
- scale()
- rotate()
- matrix()
- skewX()
- skewY()

The translate() method

The translate method is used to move an element from the current position to another.

This example shows how you can move an element 70 pixels to the right and 120 pixels down from its position:

```
<!DOCTYPE html>
<html>
<head>
<style>
div {
    width: 200px;
    height: 80px;
    background-color: orange;
    border: 2px solid black;
    -ms-transform: translate(70px,120px); /*Internet Explorer 9*/
    -webkit-transform: translate(70px,120px); /*Safari*/
    transform: translate(70px,120px); /*Standard syntax*/
}
</style>
</head>
<body>

<div>
The translate() method was used to move this <div> element from its position to
70 pixels to the right and 120 pixels down.
</div>

</body>
</html>
```

223

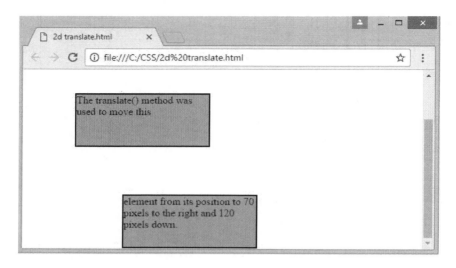

The rotate() method

The rotate() method is used to rotate an element clockwise or counter-clockwise. A positive value rotates the element clockwise while a negative value rotates it counter-clockwise.

Here's a code that rotates an element 35 degrees clockwise:

```
<!DOCTYPE html>
<html>
  <head>
    <style>
      div {
        width: 250px;
        height: 120px;
        background-color: green;
        border: 2px solid blue;
        }

      div#Div2 {
      -ms-transform: rotate(35deg); /*IE9*/
      -webkit-transform: rotate(35deg); /*Safari*/
      transform: rotate(35deg); /*Standard*/
      }
  </style>
</head>
```

224

```
<body>

  <div>
    A div element in its normal position
  </div>

  <div id="Div2">
    A div element that had been rotated 35 degrees clockwise
  </div>

</body>
</html>
```

Here's the result:

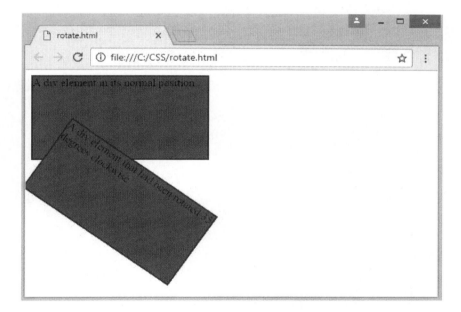

The scale() Method

The scale() method can be used to increase or decrease an element's size.

The standard syntax is transform: scale(x, y); where x refers to the increase in width and y to the increase in height.

225

For example, if you want to increase the width to three times its original width and the height to two times the original height:

transform: scale(3, 2);

On the other hand, if you want to decrease the width and height to half of their original values:

transform: scale(.5, .5);

Here's an example:

```
<!DOCTYPE html>
  <html>
    <head>
      <style>
        div {
          margin: 180px;
          width: 150px;
          height: 80px;
          background-color: green;
          border: 2px solid red;
          border: 2px solid red;
          -ms-transform: scale(3,2);
          -webkit-transform: scale(3,2);
          transform: scale(3,2);
          }
      </style>
    </head>
    <body>

    <p>The scale() method</p>

      <div>
      A div element which is three times its original width and two times its
original height
      </div>

    </body>
</html>
```

The skewX() Method

The skewX() method is used to skew an element along the X-axis.

This code skews the element 35 degrees along the X-axis:

```
<html>
  <head>
    <style>
        div {
        width: 250px;
        height: 120px;
        background-color: green;
        border: 2px solid blue;
        }

        div#Div1 {
        -ms-transform: skewX(35deg);
        -webkit-transform: skewX(35deg);
        transform: skewX(35deg);
        }
    </style>
  </head>
  <body>
```

227

```
<p>The skewX() method</p>

<div>
  A regular div element
</div>

<div id="Div1">
  A skewed div element
</div>

  </body>
</html>
```

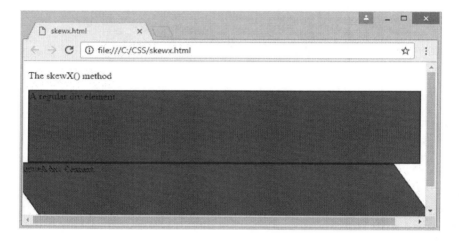

The skewY() Method

The skew(Y) method is used to skew an object along the Y-axis.

Here's an example:

```
<!DOCTYPE html>
<html>
  <head>
    <style>
        div {
        width: 250px;
        height: 120px;
        background-color: green;
        border: 2px solid blue;
```

228

```
            }

        div#Div1 {
        -ms-transform: skewY(35deg);
        -webkit-transform: skewY(35deg);
        transform: skewY(35deg);
        }
    </style>
  </head>
  <body>

    <p>The skewY() method</p>

    <div>
      A regular div element
    </div>

    <div id="Div1">
      A skewed div element
    </div>

  </body>
</html>
```

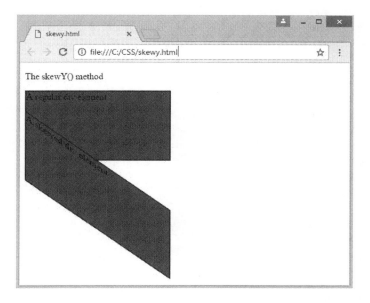

The skew() Method

The skew() method is used when you want to skew an element along both the X and Y axis.

For example, this code skews an element along the X-axis at 25 degrees and along the Y-axis at 15 degrees:

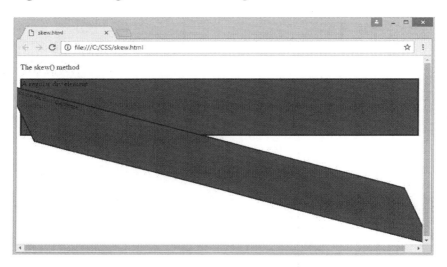

The matrix() Method

The matrix() method allows you to combine all 2D transform methods in a single element. It takes six parameters that allow you to scale, skew, and translate the X and Y axis.

Here's the syntax:

matrix(scaleX(),skewY(),skewX(),scaleY(),translateX(),translateY())

Example:

```
<!DOCTYPE html>
 <html>
  <head>
   <style>
```

```
    div {
      width: 250px;
      height: 80px;
      border: 2px solid green;
      background-color: pink;
      }

    div#Div1 {
      -ms-transform: matrix(0.5, -0.2, 0, 2, 0, 0);
      -webkit-transform: matrix(0.5, -0.2, 0, 2, 0, 0);
      transform: matrix(0.5, -0.2, 0, 2, 0, 0);
      }

    div#Div2 {
      -ms-transform: matrix(2, 0.5, 0.5, 2, 95, 0);
      -webkit-transform: matrix(2, 0.5, 0.5, 2, 95, 0);
      transform: matrix(2, 0.5, 0.5, 2, 95, 0);
      }
  </style>
</head>
<body>

  <p>The matrix() method</p>

<div>
  A regular div element
</div>

<div id="Div1">
  Matrix() Method Figure 1
</div>

<div id="Div2">
  Matrix() Method Figure 2
</div>

</body>
</html>
```

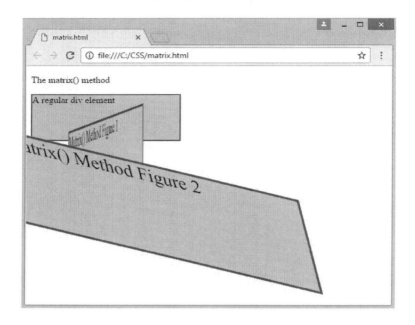

3D Transformation

CSS3 now lets you format your elements using 3D transformation with several transformation methods:

Method	Defines:
rotateX(angle)	3D rotation along X-axis
rotateY(angle)	3D rotation along the Y-axis
rotateZ(angle)	3D rotation along the Z-axis
rotate3d(x,y,z,angle)	a 3D rotation
translate3d(x,y,z)	3D translation
translateX(x)	3D translation with only the X-axis value
translateY(y)	3D translation with only the Y-axis value
translateZ(z)	3D translation with only the Z-axis value

scale3d(x,y,z)	3D scale transformation
scaleX(x)	3D scale transformation with only the X-axis value
scaleY(y)	3D scale transformation with only the Y-axis value
scaleZ(z)	3D scale transformation with only the Z-axis value
rotate3d(x,y,z,angle)	3D rotation
perspective(n)	perspective view for 3D transformed elements
matrix3d(n,n,n,n,n,n, n,n,n,n,n,n,n,n,n,n)	3D transformation with 4x4 matrix of values

The rotate() method is used to rotate an element around the X-axis.

The following example will demonstrate how the rotateX() method is used to rotate a div element to 180 degrees around the X-axis:

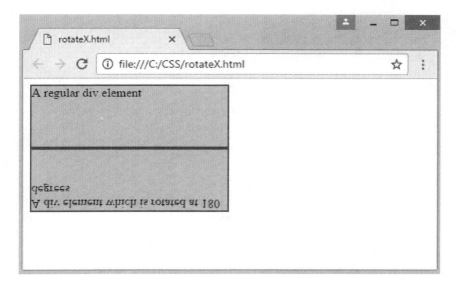

Transitions

CSS3 transitions lets you change smoothly from one property value to another for a specified duration.

To create transition effects in CSS3, you must define the following:

- the CSS property
- the effect's duration

For example, the following code causes the specified property, width, to extend for three seconds when a user hovers over the element:

```
<!DOCTYPE html>
<html>
  <head>
    <style>
      div {
          width: 125px;
          height: 125px;
          background: green;
          -webkit-transition: width 3s;
          transition: width 3s;
          }

      div:hover {
          width: 250px;
          }
    </style>
  </head>
  <body>

    <div></div>

    <p>The element extends its width when you hover over it.</p>

  </body>
</html>
```

Here's how it may look:

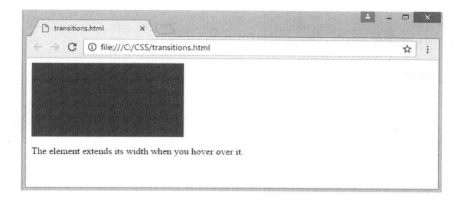

The element extends its width when you hover over it.

Animations

Animation involves creating motions and shape changes with elements. Animation effects allow the elements to gradually change between styles. CSS lets you animate most HTML elements without the need for Flash or Javascript.

The @keyframes

To use it, you must first define keyframes which control the animation steps and hold the styles that an element will have at specific times.

For the animation to work, you have to bind it to the element.

Here is an example of an animation code:

```
@keyframes trial {
    from {background-color: blue;}
    to {background-color: green;}
    }
```

The following code segment specifies the element to which the animation will apply:

```
div {
    width: 100px;
    height: 100px;
```

```
background-color: blue;
animation-name: trial;
animation-duration: 3s;
}
```

Take note that you have to specify the duration before the animation settings can take effect.

Here's an example:

```
<!DOCTYPE html>
<html>
<head>
<style>
div {
    width: 80px;
    height: 80px;
    background-color: blue;
    -webkit-animation-name: trial;
    -webkit-animation-duration: 4s;
    animation-name: trial;
    animation-duration: 3s;
}

@-webkit-keyframes example {
    from {background-color: blue;}
    to {background-color: green;}
}

@keyframes example {
    from {background-color: blue;}
    to {background-color: green;}
}
</style>
</head>
<body>


<div></div>

</body>
</html>
```

Flexbox

CSS3 introduced a new layout mode called flexbox or flexible boxes. It is used to control the elements and allow the page layout to accommodate different display devices and screen sizes.

A flexbox is made up of flex containers and items. A flex container can have more than one flex items.

You can declare a flex container by setting the element's display property to flex or inline-flex. Flex items are placed along a flex line of a flex container. The default position is horizontal from left to right.

The following example shows a flex container with three flex items:

```
<!DOCTYPE html>
<html>
<head>
<style>
.flex-container {
    display: flex;
    width: 300px;
    height: 200px;
    background-color: gold;
}

.flex-item {
    background-color: green;
    width: 80px;
    height: 80px;
    margin: 12px;
}
</style>
</head>
<body>

<div class="flex-container">
  <div class="flex-item">Item no. 1</div>
  <div class="flex-item">Item no. 2</div>
  <div class="flex-item">Item no. 3</div>
</div>

</body>
</html>
```

Here's what the browser will display:

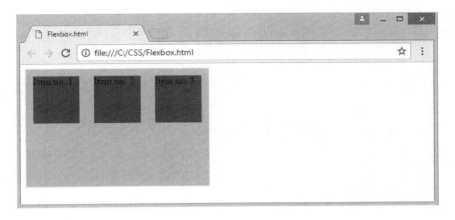

Styling Buttons

The following code will show a basic button design:

```
<!DOCTYPE html>
<html>
<head>
<style>
.button {
    background-color: #DEB887;
    border: 1px solid black;
    color: white;
    padding: 10px 30px;
    text-decoration: none;
        text-align: center;
    display: inline-block;
    font-size: 18px;
    margin: 2px 1px;
    cursor: pointer;
}
</style>
</head>
<body>

<h1>Basic Buttons</h1>
```

```
<button>Default Button</button>
<a href="#" class="button">Edit Button</a>
<button class="button">Link Button</button>
<button class="button">Input Button</button>
</body>
</html>
```

Changing the Font Size

You can use the font-size property to change the button's font size.

Here's an example:

```
<head>
<style>
.button {
    background-color: Grey;
    border: none;
    color: white;
    padding: 20px 35px;
    text-decoration: none;
    text-align: center;
    display: inline-block;
    margin: 3px 1px;
    cursor: pointer;
}

.button1 {font-size: 22px;}
.button2 {font-size: 18px;}
.button3 {font-size: 12px;}
.button4 {font-size: 25px;}
```

```
.button5 {font-size: 10px;}
</style>
</head>
<body>

<h2>Button Font Sizes</h2>

<button class="button button1">Link (22px)</button>
<button class="button button2">Search (18px)</button>
<button class="button button3">Back (12px)</button>
<button class="button button4">Input (25px)</button>
<button class="button button5">Exit (10px)</button>
</body>
```

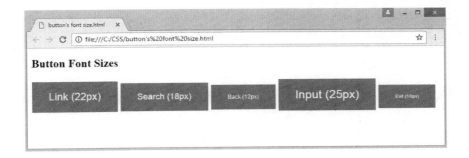

User Interface

CSS3 lets you transform an element into a user interface element with User Interface.

The following are the properties that you can use to change elements into interface ones:

appearance	allows you to create a new user interface element from other elements
box-sizing	used for fixing elements on area
resize	allows elements to be resized
outline-offset	used to add space between the outline and the element's borders or edge

241

nav-index	used to set an element's tab order
nav-down	used to specify document navigation when using the arrow down key
nav-up	used to specify document navigation when using the arrow down key
nav-left	used to specify document navigation when using the left arrow key
nav-right	use to specify document navigation using the right arrow key

Resize Property

This property is used to set whether or not a user can resize elements. You can use the values horizontal, vertical, or both to specify whether the user can adjust an element's width, height, or both.

For example, to allow the user to adjust a <div> element's width, you can use the horizontal value. Here's the code:

```
div {
   resize:horizontal;
   overflow:auto;
    }
```

To allow the user to adjust the <div> element's height, you can use the vertical value:

```
div {
    resize:vertical;
   overflow:auto;
    }
```

You can also allow the user to adjust both the width and the height using the 'both' value:

```
div {
  resize:both;
  overflow:auto;
    }
```

Outline-Offset

This property creates a space between the outline and the element's border/edge.

Take note that outline is different from the borders. It refers to the line drawn around an element and may or may not be rectangular. Likewise, it doesn't require space.

For example, this code adds a 20px space between the outline and the <div> element's border:

```
div {
    border:1px solid gray;
    outline:1px solid green;
    outline-offset:20px;
```

Box Sizing

This CSS3 property lets you include borders and padding in the total height and width of an element.

The default height and width of an element is computed using this formula:

total width: width + border + padding
total height: height + border + padding

This translates to bigger height and width figures for the element as the figures for both padding and border have to be added to the given height or width of the element. Web designers had to set smaller height and width values to accommodate the additional figures.

CSS3 introduced the box-sizing feature to address this issue. It facilitates the inclusion of the border and padding in the total height and width of an element.

This property can be accessed with this syntax:

box-sizing:border-box;

Here's how you can apply box sizing to an element:

```
.div4{
    height: 200px;
    width: 250px;
    border: 1px solid green;
    box-sizing: border-box;
}

.div5 {
    height: 200px;
    width: 250px;
    padding: 20px;
    border: 1px solid blue;
    box-sizing:border-box;
}
```

The above code will result in the same box size for div4 and div5.

CONCLUSION:

Thanks again for downloading and reading this book. I'm confident that you have gained the important skills you need to build and design a great looking, user-friendly, and web-friendly website on your own. You can use these skills to create or customize your own website or offer your services to help other people build and style theirs. I hope that you will continue to learn and practice what you have learned. May you achieve the objectives that you have set for yourself.

OTHER BOOKS BY ICODE ACADEMY

If you want to know more about other books from the series, click on the link in each title:

Book 1 : Python For Beginners: Your Guide To Easily Learn Python Programming in 7 Days

Book 2 : <u>Programming For Beginners: 3 Manuscripts in 1 Bundle - Python For Beginners, Java Programming and Html & CSS For Beginners</u>

Book 3: <u>**HTML & CSS For Beginners: Your Step by Step Guide to Easily HtmL & Css Programming in 7 Days**</u>

Book 4: <u>C Programming for Beginners: Your Guide to Easily Learn C Programming In 7 Days</u>

Book 5: JQuery For Beginners: Your Guide To Easily Learn Jquery Programming in 7 Days

Book 6: HTML5 and CSS3 for Beginners: Your Guide To Easily Learn Html5 and Css3 in 7 Days

Book 7: Ruby For Beginners: Your Guide To Easily Learn Html5 and Css3 in 7 Days

DID YOU ENJOY THIS BOOK?

I want to thank you for purchasing and reading this book. I really hope you got a lot out of it.

Can I ask a quick favor though?

If you enjoyed this book I would really appreciate it if you could leave me a positive review on Amazon.
I love getting feedback from my customers and reviews on Amazon really do make a difference. I read all my reviews and would really appreciate your thoughts.
Thanks so much.

The ICode Academy

p.s. You can click here to go directly to the book on Amazon and leave your review.

Made in the USA
Columbia, SC
17 April 2018